MFL
AS/A Level

Oxford
Literature
Companions

# La casa de Bernarda Alba



FEDERICO GARCÍA LORCA

*Notes and activities:*
*Margaret Bond and Lorenzo Moya Morallón*

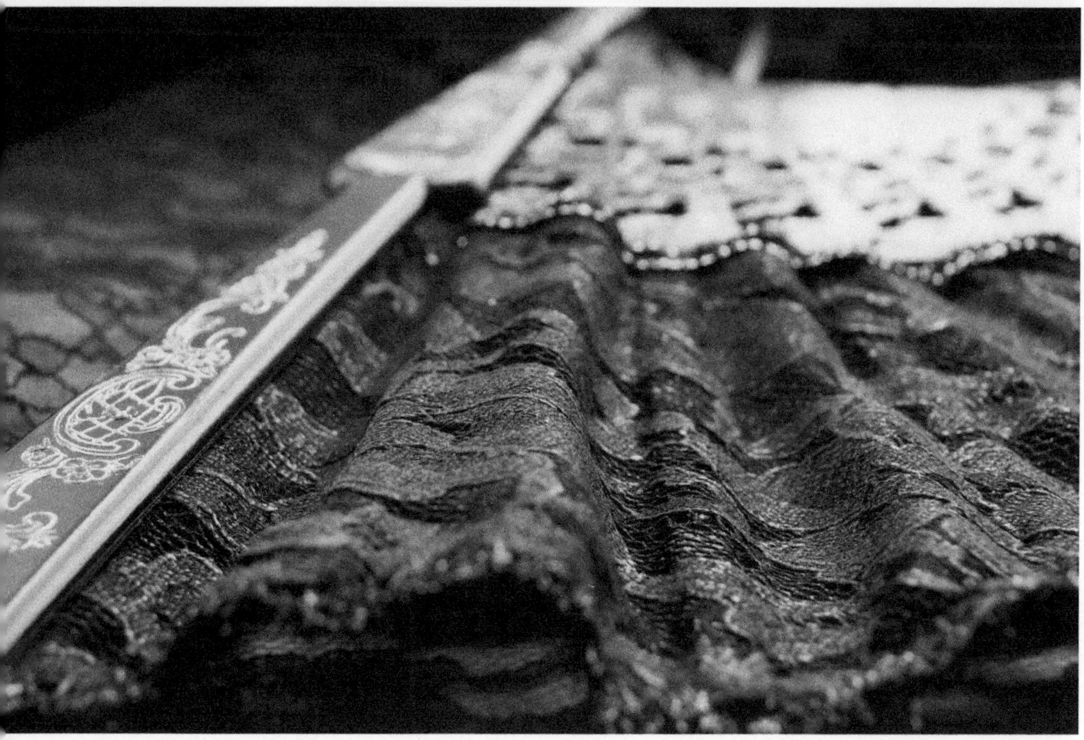

OXFORD
UNIVERSITY PRESS

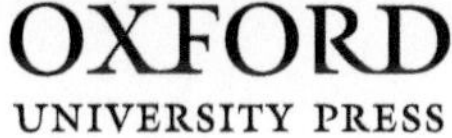

# Contents

# Introduction

## What are Oxford Literature Companions?

The Oxford Literature Companions (MFL) series is designed to provide you with comprehensive support for popular set texts. You can use the Companion alongside your play, using relevant sections during your studies or using the book as a whole for revision.

Each Companion includes detailed guidance and practical activities on:

- **Plot and Structure**
- **Context**
- **Characters**
- **Language**
- **Themes**
- **Skills and Practice**

## How does this book help with exam preparation?

As well as providing guidance on key areas of the play, throughout this book you will also find 'Upgrade' features. These are tips to help with your exam preparation and performance.

In addition, the **Skills and Practice** chapter provides detailed guidance on areas such as how to prepare for the exam, understanding the question, planning your response and hints for what to do (or not do) in the exam. There is also a bank of **Sample questions** and **Sample answers**. The **Sample answers** are marked and include annotations and a summative comment.

## How does this book help with terminology?

Throughout the book, key terms are **highlighted** in the text and explained on the page with the equivalent term in Spanish. The same terms are also included in a detailed **Glossary** at the end of the book.

## Which edition of the play has this book used?

Quotations have been taken from the Bloomsbury Methuen Drama edition of *La casa de Bernarda Alba* (ISBN 978-0-7136-8677-7).

Regarding quotations: Federico García Lorca uses the traditional accent on demonstrative pronouns, for example 'ésta'. All spellings in quotations have been kept as in the original text.

## How does this book work?

Each book in the Oxford Literature Companions (MFL) series follows the same approach and includes the following features:

- **Key quotations** from the play
- **Key terms** explained on the page in English with Spanish translations, linked to a complete glossary at the end of the book
- **Activity boxes** with activities in Spanish to help improve your understanding of the text and language skills, including:
  - Vocabulary activities
  - Comprehension activities
  - Summary activities
  - Grammar activities
  - Translation activities
  - Research activities
- **Upgrade** tips to help prepare you for your assessment
- **Vocabulary and useful phrases** in Spanish at the end of each chapter to aid your revision.

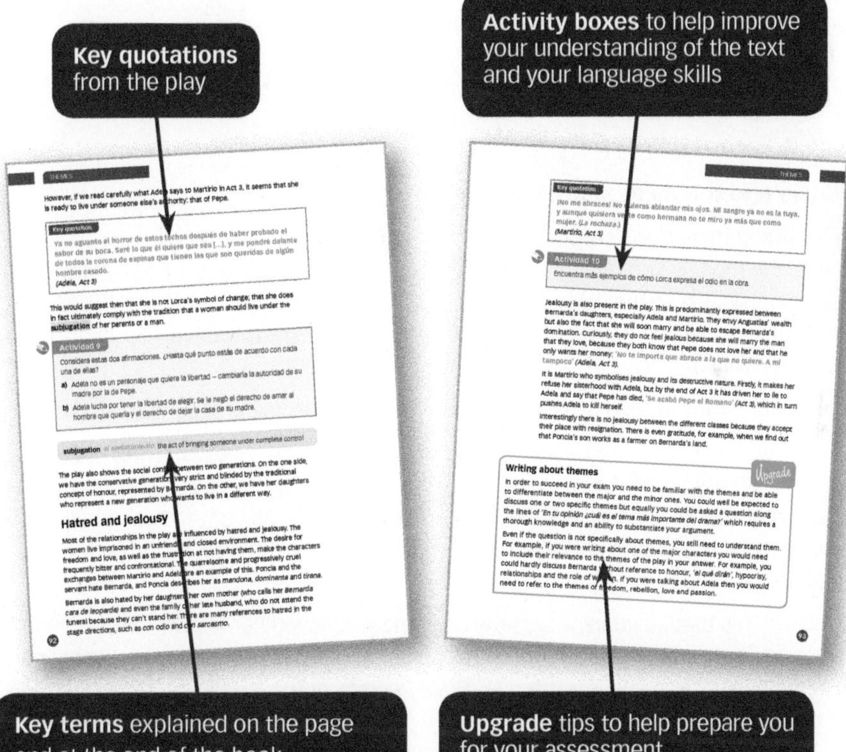

# Plot and Structure

Before starting to read the play, a glance through the list of characters will provide useful information: we learn that the **eponymous** character Bernarda has five daughters and a mother. We learn their ages and we note that the cast is made up entirely of female characters. Also on this initial page there is an announcement from the author *(el poeta)* that his intention is for the three acts of the play to be a photographic **documentary**: *El poeta advierte que estos tres actos tienen la intención de un documental fotográfico.*

Different editions of the play contain some variation in the ages attributed to the daughters. This study guide is based on the Methuen Parallel English and Spanish texts edition where the ages are given as: Angustias (39), Magdalena (30), Amelia (27), Martirio (24) and Adela (20).

Upgrade

### Tips for assessment

Make sure that you know who's who in the play! It is important to be able to differentiate between the five daughters.

## Plot

### Act 1

#### Poncia and the maid set the scene

In his **stage directions** Lorca has been very precise in his requirements for the scene: the room is *very* white, with thick walls, and its furnishings (which indicate that the residents of the house are relatively well-to-do) are specified: **'Habitación blanquísima... Muros gruesos... cortinas de yute rematadas con madroños y volantes'** *(Act 1).*

The scene begins in silence as the curtain rises and then the church bells are heard.

The maid enters, followed by the housekeeper (Poncia). In this **exposition**, the two servants set the scene for us – a technique frequently used by classical playwrights. It is from these two characters that we discover that the man of the house has died and that his funeral has been taking place; during the funeral his daughter Magdalena fainted.

Poncia states that Magdalena was the only one who loved her father: **'Era la única que quería al padre'** *(Act 1).* (Note: This phrasing is the accepted version, although in some editions the line is written as '*Era a la única que quería el padre*' which changes the meaning significantly.)

The servants' ensuing conversation paints a vivid portrait of Bernarda. Poncia describes her in unfavourable terms: **'¡Mandona! ¡Dominanta! [...] ¡Tirana de los que la rodean!'** *(Act 1)*. This introduces the themes of bitterness and **antipathy** which go through the whole play. We also learn about Bernarda's obsession with cleanliness.

It becomes clear that the mother of Bernarda is locked away and that only Bernarda's relatives are attending the funeral as her husband's family hates her.

As the church bells resume their ringing, Poncia goes to hear the **last response** because she likes to hear the priest sing. You will recall that in the opening scene we heard that Magdalena had fainted at ***'el primer responso'***. At some point after this, Poncia left the church to go back to the house to get some food, chatted to the maid and then said she was going back to hear ***'el último responso'***, which shows that the funeral service was very long.

- Bernarda's second husband has recently died and his funeral is taking place.
- Bernarda's personality comes across from the conversation between Poncia and the maid.
- We find out that Bernarda has five unmarried daughters.
- Only the daughter of the first husband has inherited a significant amount of money, which will become a source of tension in the play.

**eponymous** *epónimo* the person after whom a literary work/film is named

**documentary** *el documental* a factual account of an event or person presenting the facts with little or no fiction

**stage directions** *las acotaciones* instructions to an actor or director, written into the script of a play

**exposition** *la exposición* dialogue or description that gives the audience or reader the background of the characters and the present situation

**antipathy** *la antipatía* a feeling of intense aversion, dislike, or hostility

**last response** *el último responso* the final part of a Mass

**Key quotation**

**Le quedan cinco mujeres, cinco hijas feas, que quitando a Angustias, la mayor, que es la hija del primer marido y tiene dineros, las demás mucha puntilla bordada, muchas camisas de hilo, pero pan y uvas por toda herencia.**

*(Poncia, Act 1)*

## Actividad 1

Rellena los huecos en las frases siguientes con un nombre u otra palabra adecuada.

**a)** Bernarda Alba tiene __________ hijas.

**b)** La __________, que se llama __________, tiene treinta y nueve años y la menor, que se llama __________, __________ veinte.

**c)** El primer marido de Bernarda era el padre de __________.

**d)** María Josefa es la __________ de Bernarda y tiene __________ años.

**e)** La primera hija de su segundo marido se llama __________.

**f)** Martirio nació tres años después de __________.

**g)** Bernarda tiene dos __________. La mayor, que se llama __________, tiene sesenta años.

### The beggar calls and the mourners return to the house

While Poncia is away, a beggar woman and her daughter come to the house asking for scraps; the beggar is sent packing by the maid, who exerts her authority over someone even lower than herself in the class structure. The maid then reveals that she had a relationship with Bernarda's late husband and is **mourning** his loss: **'Yo fui la que más te quiso de las que te sirvieron. ¿Y he de vivir yo después de haberte marchado? ¿Y he de vivir?'** *(Act 1).*

The mourners start to enter the house, all carrying black fans.

As Bernarda and her daughters enter, Bernarda shouts **'¡Silencio!'**, her first word in the play. She sends the maid away sobbing, and makes the comment **'Los pobres son como los animales. Parece como si estuvieran hechos de otras sustancias'** *(Act 1).*

Bernarda then shouts at Magdalena to stop crying, and the conversation moves on to farming matters. The men who have attended the funeral are left in the courtyard and sent lemonade with the warning from Bernarda that they are not to enter the house.

There is a first mention of Pepe el Romano when a girl says that he was with the mourners, although Bernarda corrects her. Bernarda criticises another woman who supposedly looked at a man in church. According to Bernarda, **'Las mujeres en la iglesia no deben mirar más hombre que al oficiante, y a ése porque tiene faldas. Volver la cabeza es buscar el calor de la pana'** *(Act 1).*

Meanwhile, other women are criticising Bernarda behind her back. Bernarda calls for a final prayer and all join in. Then she shoos away a girl who attempts to offer comfort to Magdalena.

As the mourners leave, Bernarda shouts after them: **'¡Andar a vuestras cuevas a criticar todo lo que habéis visto!'** *(Act 1),* expressing her contempt that they will now go away talking about her unfavourably.

**Key quotation**

**MUJER 1** *(en voz baja.)* **¡Vieja lagarta recocida!**

**PONCIA** *(entre dientes.)* **¡Sarmentosa por calentura de varón!**
*(Act 1)*

## Actividad 2

Traduce al inglés el siguiente texto que resume la primera parte del primer acto.

La obra comienza con una conversación entre las dos criadas de Bernarda mientras preparan la casa para recibir a los dolientes después de la misa por el difunto marido de Bernarda. A través de su charla empezamos a conocer a su tiránica y autoritaria dueña. La criada mayor, Poncia, se va a la iglesia para oír el último responso y en su ausencia viene a la casa una mendiga, pidiendo las sobras pero la criada menor la trata con desdén.

Al terminar la misa, las vecinas entran en la casa pero los hombres tienen que permanecer fuera porque Bernarda no quiere que pasen adentro. Las mujeres cotillean sobre Bernarda y sus hijas y cuando se despiden de Bernarda, ésta les insulta.

## Bernarda reveals the mourning period of eight years

Now alone with her daughters and Poncia, Bernarda asks Adela for a fan but is horrified to be given her red and green one and throws it on the floor, accusing her daughter of disrespect: '**¿Es éste el abanico que se da a una viuda? Dame uno negro y aprende a respetar el luto de tu padre**' *(Act 1)*.

Bernarda then delivers the news to her daughters that they will endure eight years of mourning: '**En ocho años que dure el luto no ha de entrar en esta casa el viento de la calle**' *(Act 1)*. During that period they will sew and embroider their **trousseaus**. This is terrible news for Bernarda's daughters as they will not be allowed outside of the house (except to go to Mass) or to be courted by men, for eight years. However, we discover subsequently that Angustias will be allowed to marry, because Antonio María Benavides was not her father. The most affected daughter is Adela, who is the youngest.

**mourning** *el luto* the conventional signs of sorrow for a person's death, especially wearing black, not leaving the house except to go to church

**trousseau** *el ajuar* a collection of belongings women take with them on marriage, including clothes and linen for their new home; usually which they will sew themselves

Although Magdalena says she will not do the embroidery, she accepts the imposed period of mourning with resignation as she believes that she will never marry. She would, however, prefer to do anything other than stay in day after day. According to Bernarda, this is what it means to be a woman – **'Eso tiene ser mujer'** *(Act 1)* – and she will have to do what her mother tells her. The role of women is considered in the section on Context (page 36).

Bernarda's elderly mother, María Josefa, is heard shouting to be let out of her locked room and Bernarda asks the maid to take her onto the patio to let off steam but not to let her go near the well, where she could be seen from neighbouring windows.

Adela tells Bernarda that Angustias has been watching men through a crack in the wall – Bernarda calls for Angustias to come to her, tells her off and hits her with her stick. Poncia tries to calm Bernarda who tells her daughters to get out.

- Bernarda violently rejects Adela's offer of her red and green fan because she considers the colours inappropriate for a widow, emphasising her obsession with tradition.
- Bernarda announces the eight-year period of mourning. It does not need to be so long but she decides to follow her family tradition in spite of her daughters' needs. The eight-year period is very long and she will have chosen it because of her obsession with *'el qué dirán'* (what people think - literally, what people will say) in order to show that she is better than the rest of the village.
- Bernarda's daughters will spend that time incarcerated, sewing and embroidering their trousseaus.

Bernarda Alba and her daughters enter a period of mourning; Timaginas Teatro, 2013

- We are made aware of the presence in the house of María Josefa, Bernarda's senile mother, who is kept locked away to protect Bernarda's reputation.
- Bernarda's cruel character is further revealed when she exhibits physical violence towards her daughter and hits her with her stick.

**Key quotation**

**Haceros cuenta que hemos tapiado con ladrillos puertas y ventanas. Así pasó en casa de mi padre y en casa de mi abuelo.**
*(Bernarda, Act 1)*

**Actividad 3**

Traduce las siguientes frases al español.

**a)** After the funeral, Bernarda was hot and Adela gave her a red and green fan. Bernarda was very angry and threw it on the floor as it was not appropriate for a widow.

**b)** Bernarda told her daughters that there would be an eight-year period of mourning.

**c)** When they heard María Josefa shouting, Bernarda told the maid to take her outside.

**d)** Bernarda didn't want her mother to go near the well because the neighbours might see her.

**e)** Bernarda was angry with Angustias because she had been seen watching the men after the funeral.

### Paca la Roseta and the discussion of Angustias' marriage

Bernarda wants to know from Poncia what the men had been talking about and is told that they were talking about Paca la Roseta who was taken to the olive grove by a group of men after they had tied up her husband. Supposedly Paca enjoyed the experience. Bernarda damns her saying she is the only loose woman in the village, but Poncia says that she is an outsider and that those who had taken her were the sons of outsiders too: **'Es la única mujer mala que tenemos en el pueblo'** *(Act 1).*

Poncia comments that none of Bernarda's daughters has had a **suitor**. Bernarda is furious, saying that there is no one suitable – not of their class.

Amelia and Martirio enter, discussing one of the neighbours, Adelaida, who wasn't at the funeral because her fiancé won't let her out of the house: **'Antes era alegre; ahora ni polvos se echa en la cara'** *(Act 1)*, which makes Amelia think that perhaps it's better to be without a suitor.

**suitor** *el pretendiente* a potential partner/spouse

Martirio gossips about Adelaida's family – because Bernarda knows their story, they are scared of her. Martirio thinks it is better to do without a man and they talk about her one-time suitor, Enrique Humanes, who left her and married a richer woman.

Magdalena comes in and says she has been looking at things in their grandmother's room. The past was happier with no gossip. She is explaining that although in some respects life in the village has become more modern, like in the towns, old traditions still remain: **'Hoy hay más finura. Las novias se ponen velo blanco como en las poblaciones, y se bebe vino de botella, pero nos pudrimos por el qué dirán'** *(Act 1).*

Magdalena tells them that Adela has gone out into the yard wearing the green dress she had made for her birthday and was telling the chickens to look at her. She also reports to the others that Angustias is going to marry Pepe el Romano – it's the talk of the village. Amelia and Magdalena say they are pleased but Martirio doesn't believe them. She says she would be happy for Angustias too if it weren't for the fact that Pepe is just marrying her for her money.

When Adela comes back in, she too is told of the impending marriage of Angustias and Pepe el Romano and she can't believe it. She complains that this period of mourning has come at the worst time in her life and she doesn't intend to go along with it: **'¡Mañana me pondré mi vestido verde y me echaré a pasear por la calle! ¡Yo quiero salir!'** *(Act 1).* We discover later on in Act 2 that Adela had a relationship with Pepe el Romano. When the maid says that Pepe el Romano is in the street, the girls rush to look out of the window to see him.

The youngest daughter Adela seems determined not to follow the rules of mourning, shown here in this production at the Almeida Theatre in London, 2012

Bernarda re-enters talking about the will. Angustias is to inherit more than the others. Angustias is told off for using make-up on the day of her father's funeral and responds angrily: **'No era mi padre. El mío murió hace tiempo. ¿Es que ya no lo recuerda usted?'***(Act 1).*

Bernarda tries to forcibly remove the make-up from Angustias' face. An argument follows between Magdalena and Angustias and then María Josefa appears on stage demanding her **mantilla** and pearl necklace, saying she wants none of her things to be Bernarda's and that none of them will get married. She says she escaped because she wants to get married on the seashore: **'¡Quiero irme de aquí! ¡Bernarda! A casarme a la orilla del mar, a la orilla del mar'** *(Act 1).*

- We hear about the scandal of Paca la Roseta and it is telling of Bernarda's character that she immediately puts the blame on her.
- Bernarda's obsession with class is shown when she says the men in the village are not good enough for her daughters.
- We find out that Martirio once had a potential suitor: Enrique Humanes.
- The girls' gossip about Adelaida reveals their disappointment with men.
- Adela wears her green dress without her mother's knowledge. This is an important **symbol** as it represents sexual desire, defiance and a longing for freedom.
- María Josefa tries to escape Bernarda's tyranny. She is the other character who is actively seeking freedom.

**mantilla** *la mantilla* a lace or silk scarf worn by women over the head and shoulders

**symbol** *el símbolo* an object used to represent an idea, often an important theme in the story

María Josefa (Marina Valverde) also strives to leave the house of Bernarda Alba; Teatro Tribueñe, 2011

**Key quotations**

**¡No, no ha tenido novio ninguna, ni les hace falta! Pueden pasarse muy bien. ... Los hombres de aquí no son de su clase. ¿Es que quieres que las entregue a cualquier gañán?**
*(Bernarda, Act 1)*

**Me escapé porque me quiero casar, porque quiero casarme con un varón hermoso de la orilla del mar, ya que aquí los hombres huyen de las mujeres.**
*(María Josefa, Act 1)*

## Actividad 4

Sin mirar el texto de la obra:

1. Empareja las dos partes de las siguientes frases de la última parte del primer acto.
2. Traduce las frases completas al inglés.
3. Menciona que personaje dice cada frase y explica las circunstancias.

| | | | |
|---|---|---|---|
| **1** | Paca la Roseta traía el pelo suelto | **a** | al tranco de la calle. |
| **2** | ¡Cuánto hay que sufrir y luchar para hacer que las personas | **b** | ni más mis anillos, ni mi traje negro de moaré, porque ninguna de vosotras se va a casar. |
| **3** | Su novio no la deja salir ni | **c** | pero sin desahogaros con nadie. |
| **4** | A ellos les importa la tierra, las yuntas | **d** | y una corona de flores en la cabeza. |
| **5** | Mejor que yo lo sabéis las dos, siempre cabeza con cabeza como dos ovejitas | **e** | y una perra sumisa que les dé de comer. |
| **6** | Nada de lo que tengo quiero que sea para vosotras, | **f** | sean decentes y no tiren al monte demasiado! |

# Act 2

### The sisters discuss Pepe el Romano

The scene is now 'white', '*Habitación blanca del interior de la casa de Bernarda*', rather than 'very white'. It has moved further into the interior of the house, with doors leading off to the bedrooms.

Except for Adela, who is in her room, the sisters are sewing; Magdalena is doing embroidery. There is bickering between Angustias and the others about the time that Pepe el Romano had left Angustias' window the previous night. Angustias said he left about 1.30 am, but Poncia says she heard him at 4.00 am which is also what Amelia thought. According to Angustias it could not have been him.

Martirio and Amelia question Angustias on what Pepe had said the first time he came to her window to begin courting her, and Martirio comments on how strange it is that the engagement happened so quickly.

Poncia tells a slightly **risqué** tale of when her husband Evaristo el Colorín first came to her window and then goes on to say how she was a strong and tough wife:

**'MARTIRIO. ¿Es verdad que le pegaste algunas veces?**

**PONCIA. Sí, y por poco lo dejo tuerto'** *(Act 2).*

They call Adela – Poncia thinks she is sick. Martirio says it's because she doesn't sleep and Angustias says it is because she is going mad with envy.

Adela enters and says she doesn't feel well – but wants no questions from Martirio who, she complains to Poncia, won't leave her alone and laments that Adela will never have a husband. Adela says to Poncia that her body will be for whoever she wants, to which Poncia replies, **'De Pepe el Romano, ¿no es eso?'** *(Act 2).* It shocks Adela to find that Poncia has guessed the situation with Pepe. Poncia confronts her about it, telling her to leave her sister in peace – Angustias won't survive the first childbirth and then Pepe will marry Adela. Poncia is showing genuine concern for Adela, but also says that she wants to live in a respectable house.

There is a quick change of subject to cover up the conversation as Angustias comes back in.

- The setting is now further in to the interior of the house, which symbolises the fact that the sisters are being cut off from the outside world.
- Tensions between the sisters mount, particularly the feelings of the others towards Angustias.
- Clues about the duplicity of Pepe are revealed with the debate about the times he visited Angustias.
- Discussion about what Pepe said the first time he came to Angustias' window reveals their speedy courtship; a slightly humorous account by Poncia of her husband provides a distraction.
- The conflict between Adela and Martirio is revealed and Poncia's shrewdness is demonstrated as she guesses Adela's love for Pepe.

**Key quotation**

**Tu hermana Angustias es una enferma. Esa no resiste el primer parto. Es estrecha de cintura, vieja, y con mi conocimiento te digo que se morirá. Entonces Pepe hará lo que hacen todos los viudos de esta tierra: se casará con la más joven, y la más hermosa, y ésa eres tú.**
*(Poncia, Act 2)*

**risqué** *atrevido* daringly close to indelicacy or impropriety

**Actividad 5**

Resume en 90 palabras lo que ha pasado hasta ahora desde el comienzo del segundo acto.

### The daughters quarrel and discuss the reapers in the field

The daughters discuss the lace which has just been purchased and there is a quarrel between Adela and Martirio. Magdalena states that she will do no sewing for any children Angustias might have.

The sounds of the men going back to work are heard. Adela comments that she too would like to go to the fields and Magdalena's response reveals a similar class consciousness to her mother's: **'¡Cada clase tiene que hacer lo suyo!'** *(Act 2)*. Poncia reports that forty or fifty harvesters have arrived, as has a woman **'vestida de lentejuelas'** *(Act 2)* who was taken to the olive grove by fifteen of the men. She relates how once she had given her son money for this as **'Los hombres necesitan estas cosas'** *(Act 2)*.

The singing of the **reapers** can be heard in the distance. Martirio tells Amelia that she had heard something in the stable yard the previous night: **'Quizá una mulilla sin desbravar'** *(Act 2)*, which is a **double entendre**, suggesting that the young, unbroken mule could be Adela.

Angustias storms in saying her photo of Pepe has been taken from under her pillow, and accuses them all. Bernarda enters and demands to know who has it. Poncia finds it in Martirio's bed. Martirio claims it was a joke and in the ensuing argument the sisters tell Angustias that Pepe has chosen her only for her money and land. The suggestion is that Martirio actually stole the photo because she is also in love with Pepe el Romano.

Bernarda quietens them down with her **'¡Silencio!'** *(Act 2)* and says that she knew this quarrel was brewing but did not expect it so soon. She sends them all away and realises that she has to get a firmer grip on the family and therefore she has to exert her power to stem the simmering discord amongst her daughters.

- Martirio and Adela bicker over the uses for the lace, which reflects their growing animosity towards each other.
- Magdalena asserts that she will do no sewing for any child of Angustias. The antagonism between the sisters has several causes – partially the inheritance but more so because this gives Angustias the opportunity to marry and escape from the house.
- They discuss the farm workers and the prostitute who has come to serve them; Poncia's revelation suggests women should simply accept men have these needs.
- There is speculation about sounds heard in the stable yard the previous night.
- Pepe is again the cause of trouble when Angustias reports that her photo of him is missing.
- This incident opens Bernarda's eyes to the growing tensions within the family.

**Key quotation**

**¡Silencio digo! Yo veía la tormenta venir, pero no creía que estallara tan pronto [...] tengo cinco cadenas para vosotras y esta casa levantada por mi padre para que ni las hierbas se enteren de mi desolación. ¡Fuera de aquí!**

*(Bernarda, Act 2)*

**reapers** *los segadores* men who gather the harvest

**double entendre** *el doble sentido* a word or phrase open to two different interpretations, one of which is usually risqué

## Actividad 6

1. Imagina que eres Angustias. Escribe un párrafo describiendo tus sentimientos al descubrir que tu foto de Pepe ha desaparecido.
2. Imagina que eres Martirio. Escribe un párrafo explicando los motivos por los que has cogido la foto de Pepe.
3. Escribe un párrafo en el que narras cómo reaccionan los otros personajes – Adela, Poncia, Bernarda y Amelia.

### Poncia warns Bernarda and the mob seize a woman

Bernarda and Poncia talk – Bernarda thinks that Angustias will have to get married straightaway so they can get Pepe out of the way of the other daughters. Poncia tells Bernarda to open her eyes to what is going on and leads her to believe that Martirio is the trouble, saying that Bernarda should have allowed her to marry Enrique Humanes instead of sending him a message telling him to keep away.

Bernarda is in denial, and doesn't think anything serious is going on. She accuses Poncia of wishing them ill. Poncia says it is Adela who should be marrying Pepe. Angustias, having overheard Poncia saying that Pepe left at 4.30 am, comes in to deny this. Bernarda resolves to keep watch.

The servant comes to tell them that there is a big crowd at the top of the street and Poncia is dispatched to find out what is happening.

Martirio and Adela talk. Adela says that she will have Pepe all to herself and that he wants her to live with him.

Poncia returns with the news that the unmarried daughter of a neighbour, la Librada, had a child but killed it to hide her shame. She had buried it under stones but some dogs found it, and now they are dragging the girl down the street intent on killing her. Bernarda and Martirio think this is the right thing to do. Adela clutches her stomach saying, '**¡No! ¡No!**' *(Act 2)*.

- We learn that it was Bernarda who deliberately ended the relationship between Martirio and Enrique Humanes.
- There are further disagreements over the time Pepe left the previous night.
- Bernarda is in denial about the true situation, building a sense of foreboding. This is important because it builds tension both amongst the characters and within the audience. It also illustrates Bernarda's blindness to reality.
- The sad account of the daughter of la Librada shocks Adela in particular. Her actions hint that Adela might be, or suspects that she is, pregnant.

**Key quotation**

**¡Ya sabré enterarme! Si las gentes del pueblo quieren levantar falsos testimonios se encontrarán con mi pedernal. No se hable de este asunto. Hay a veces una ola de fango que levantan los demás para perdernos.**
*(Bernarda, Act 2)*

## Actividad 7

Básate en el episodio de la mujer 'vestida de lentejuelas' (página 62) y en el relato de lo que le pasó a la hija de la Librada para escribir un párrafo de unas 90 palabras sobre la hipocresía que existe entre los diferentes códigos morales que se les atribuyen a los hombres y a las mujeres.

## Actividad 8

Pon en orden cronológico (1-8) los siguientes eventos del segundo acto.

| | | |
|---|---|---|
| **a** | Angustias se da cuenta de que su foto de Pepe ha desaparecido y acusa a sus hermanas de su robo. | |
| **b** | Se enteran de que la hija de la Librada ha tenido un hijo al que ha matado y que van a matarla a ella. | |
| **c** | Descubren que una vez Martirio tuvo la posibilidad de casarse con Enrique. | |
| **d** | Hay una fuerte discusión entre Martirio y Adela sobre sus relaciones con Pepe. | |
| **e** | Las hermanas cosen y hablan sobre la extraña conducta de Adela. | |
| **f** | Llegan los segadores. | |
| **g** | Martirio dice que la había cogido porque quería gastar una broma. | |
| **h** | Bernarda se da cuenta de que Angustias tendrá que casarse muy pronto. | |

## Actividad 9

Traduce las siguientes frases al español.

**a)** The sisters are sewing Angustias' trousseau.

**b)** Angustias knows that her sisters are jealous of her.

**c)** Poncia suspects that Adela is also in love with Pepe and that she sees him at night after he has left Angustias' window.

**d)** Adela longs for the freedom that men have.

**e)** Bernarda orders Poncia to find the missing photograph.

**f)** Bernarda and Martirio agree that the daughter of la Librada should be killed.

## Actividad 10

Rellena los huecos con la forma correcta del presente de los verbos del cuadro de abajo.

El Acto Segundo se [1]____________ en una habitación del interior de la casa.

Las hermanas y Poncia [2]____________ sábanas para la boda de Angustias.

Angustias [3]____________ de la primera conversación que tuvo con Pepe y Poncia [4]____________ la suya con su marido.

Oyen a los segadores que [5]____________ de los campos y Adela [6]____________ su libertad.

Cuando Angustias [7]____________ la desaparición de su foto, Bernarda [8]________.

Para castigar a Martirio, Bernarda la [9]____________ con su bastón.

Bernarda cree que el robo de la foto fue una broma pero Poncia [10]____________ en que pasa algo muy serio.

Adela se [11]____________ con la hija de la Librada y no [12]____________ que la maten.

| | | | |
|---|---|---|---|
| **a)** anunciar | **b)** desarrollar | **c)** envidiar | **d)** hablar |
| **e)** hacer | **f)** golpear | **g)** identificar | **h)** insistir |
| **i)** intervenir | **j)** querer | **k)** recordar | **l)** volver |

## Act 3

The act begins, as usual, with stage directions. The author explains that the action will take place in the evening in the courtyard where the family and a visitor, Prudencia, are just finishing dinner.

### Actividad 11

Este es el último de los tres actos de la obra. En cada acto las acotaciones nos dan una descripción de un lugar diferente de la casa de Bernarda. También mencionan el color de las paredes y cómo se hacen progresivamente más oscuras.

1. Lee todas las acotaciones al comienzo de cada acto y considéralas detenidamente.
2. Escribe al menos cinco puntos explicando lo que Lorca pretendía al cambiar los lugares donde se desarrolla la acción y explica con tus propias palabras por qué las paredes se vuelven más oscuras.

### Dinner with Prudencia

Prudencia is the first one to talk, saying that she is leaving, because that she has spent enough time with Bernarda and her family and wants to pray the **rosary** at church. However, Bernarda convinces her to stay a little bit longer and the conversation resumes. Prudencia talks about her family problems, the main one being that she is sad because her daughter disobeyed her father and he has not forgiven her, but Bernarda supports this: **'Es un verdadero hombre'** *(Act 3)*. As a warning, she declares that a disobedient daughter is no longer a daughter: **'Una hija que desobedece deja de ser hija para convertirse en enemiga'** *(Act 3)*.

They are loudly interrupted by the **stallion** locked in Bernarda's stable. He is kicking the walls because he has sensed the presence of the mares; it is probably hot and he wants to be free. At this moment, Prudencia praises Bernarda because she has been able to increase her stable, and in doing so, her wealth: **'Has sabido acrecentar tu ganado'** *(Act 3)*.

The stallion kicks the walls once more and they let him out as they fear he might break the walls down in his desire to be free. The stallion is a symbol of lust and freedom; he is kicking against the walls of the house, which are another symbol: of repression and incarceration. The house can be considered the **antithesis** of the stallion.

**rosary** *el rosario* a series of Catholic prayers repeated in a set order, often using rosary beads to keep track of the prayers

**stallion** *el caballo garañón* an uncastrated adult male horse, especially one used for breeding

**antithesis** *la antítesis* the direct opposite

Adela tries to leave the table to drink some water, but a jug of cold water is brought to her and she has to sit back down. Prudencia talks about the future wedding between Angustias and Pepe el Romano; she asks for Angustias to show her the engagement ring and is surprised to find out that it has three pearls instead of diamonds, saying that in her time pearls meant tears: **'Es precioso. Tres perlas. En mi tiempo las perlas significaban lágrimas'** *(Act 3).*

We find out that Pepe el Romano will come to the house to ask for Angustias' hand in marriage in three days' time. This is a particular custom when the man will formally ask his future parents-in-law for permission to marry his fiancée. Pepe has already asked and been accepted by Angustias in private, which explains why she is wearing a ring. After that, they talk about the furniture that Bernarda has bought for Angustias' wedding, about its price (quite expensive), and they also mention the wardrobe with the mirror: a novelty for them, as Bernarda and Prudencia had a chest when they each married.

Another stage direction lets us know that some distant church bells can be heard, signalling the last call for the rosary. Prudencia bids them farewell and says that she will come back to have a look at Angustias' trousseau. At this point, Adela tries again to leave the table and shows her annoyance when Amelia and Martirio decide to follow her: **ADELA. *(con odio contenido).* 'No me voy a perder'** *(Act 3).* We don't know it yet but later on it will be clear that Adela was trying to sneak off to see Pepe el Romano.

- In this section, Prudencia, one of Bernarda's neighbours, is visiting and having dinner with the women.
- They talk about Prudencia's problems and the preparations for Angustias' wedding. Angustias' ring is hinted at as an omen of future unhappiness with Pepe.
- Prudencia displays a more reasonable attitude than Bernarda, who supports Prudencia's husband and his tough rules, illustrating how women themselves sometimes perpetuated the traditional idea that women were subservient to men.
- The stallion, an important symbol of the play, keeps kicking the walls because he wants to be free and reach the mares.
- Bernarda declares that he should be released and the mares locked up – a parallel of the position her daughters are placed in.
- Adela tries to sneak out with the excuse of being thirsty, a metaphor for her thirst for desire.

**Key quotation**

***(levantándose furiosa).* ¿Hay que decir las cosas dos veces? ¡Echadlo que se revuelque en los montones de paja! … Pues encerrad las potras en la cuadra, pero dejadlo libre, no sea que eche abajo las paredes.**
*(Bernarda, Act 3)*

**Actividad 12**

Realiza un diagrama radial para ilustrar las acciones de los personajes (Prudencia, Bernarda, Adela, Amelia, Martirio, Angustias) durante la visita de Prudencia.

## Angustias confides in Bernarda

When they leave, Bernarda tells Angustias to make peace with her sister Martirio over her hiding Pepe's picture, saying that it was only a prank. Angustias replies saying she knows that her sister does not love her. Bernarda is adamant as she wants to have a respectable appearance and harmony inside the house. Then Angustias confides her troubles to her mother. She finds Pepe el Romano distracted when he talks to her and will not tell her what worries him: **'Si le pregunto qué le pasa, me contesta: 'Los hombres tenemos nuestras preocupaciones''** *(Act 3)*. She also reveals that she does not feel happy, as a soon-to-be-married woman should feel: **'Debía estar contenta y no lo estoy'** *(Act 3)*.

However, Bernarda's answer is firm and lacks any motherly instinct. She explains to Angustias that none of that matters, that she must never ask a man any questions and that she should never cry in front of him. Angustias then says that Pepe has gone to the city with his own mother and Bernarda feels relieved as she will be able to have a peaceful night. At this moment, Adela, Martirio and Amelia return. Amelia and Adela say what a dark night it is and Martirio makes a comment, saying that it is a good night for a thief, or for someone who needs to hide: **'Una buena noche para ladrones, para el que necesite escondrijo'** *(Act 3)*.This comment is intended for her younger sister, as she knows full well what her intentions are. Martirio suspects her younger sister is seeing Pepe el Romano, who comes to see Adela after having been with Angustias. Although they all think Pepe is away in the city with his mother, Martirio is being vigilant. Adela mentions the white stallion, which symbolises sexual desire and freedom, but in this instance is a **foreshadowing** of death: Adela's death. Amelia compares the white stallion to a ghost.

They talk about the stars and how Adela is in awe when she sees them shining high in the sky and how she likes shooting stars, but Martirio says she is only interested in what goes on inside the house.

- Bernarda talks to Angustias because she wants her to make peace with her sister Martirio. For Bernarda, it is very important to give the appearance of a family that gets on well.
- Angustias confides in her mother about her doubts regarding Pepe, but Bernarda dismisses them completely. Marriage for her is a duty.

- Pepe's supposed absence lulls Bernarda into a false sense of security.
- Martirio has suspicions about her sister's intentions for that night. She thinks Pepe will come but only to be with Adela.
- The white stallion foreshadows the tragedy that will unfold at the end of the play.

**foreshadowing** *el presagio* a warning of a future event

**Key quotation**

**ADELA. El caballo garañón estaba en el centro del corral ¡Blanco! Doble de grande, llenando todo lo oscuro.**

**AMELIA. Es verdad. Daba miedo. ¡Parecía una aparición!**
*(Act 3)*

## Bernarda and Poncia are alone

The girls go to bed leaving Poncia and Bernarda behind. Bernarda enjoys the silence and is quick to tell Poncia that everything is fine with her girls and that her vigilance over her daughters has ensured peace and tranquillity: **'Mi vigilancia lo puede todo'** *(Act 3)*. She enquires if Poncia's son is still talking to Pepe el Romano: **'¿Siguen diciendo todavía la mala letanía de esta casa?'** *(Act 3)* and is pleased when Poncia confirms that they do not say anything negative about her household.

Poncia still tries to warn Bernarda not to be complacent; she tries to explain that something unexpected could happen at any point, for example, maybe a bolt of lightening will strike, or a blood clot will stop her heart, but Bernarda refuses to pay any attention and goes to bed.

When Bernarda is out of the room, Poncia and the servant talk freely about how proud Bernarda is and about how she prefers to ignore all the signs rather than face them. Poncia also reveals that Pepe el Romano was pursuing Adela the previous year and that she was mad about him: **'el año pasado anduvo detrás de Adela, y ésta estaba loca por él...'** *(Act 3)*.

Poncia also fears that things have gone too far: Adela's mind is made up and the rest of the girls are watchful, especially Martirio, whose secret, unrequited love for Pepe has made her bitter and vengeful.

The sound of dogs barking makes them wonder what is going on and at that point Adela appears saying she needs a glass of water. After they leave, María Josefa makes an appearance; she is carrying a lamb with her and talks to herself about wanting to go to the seashore. Martirio finds her and convinces her to go to bed and María Josefa tells her she wants to have more children, and warns her that Pepe el Romano will devour all of them: **'Todas lo queréis. Pero él os va a devorar, porque vosotras sois granos de trigo'** *(Act 3)*.

Martirio goes back to the stable-yard door and looks for Adela. She is there and confesses to Martirio her love and devotion for Pepe el Romano, how she is madly in love with him and ready to do anything, even becoming his lover and accepting her fate. But Martirio is incensed; she is jealous of Adela and tells her so. She also confesses her love for Pepe: '**¡Sí! Déjame que el pecho se me rompa como una granada de amargura. ¡Lo quiero!**' *(Act 3)*. Neither of them mind that Pepe only wants to marry Angustias to get her money.

- In this section, we can see Bernarda's obsession with how outsiders view her family, and the importance of being well-respected.
- Poncia tries to warn Bernarda about the situation in the house but she doesn't want to listen to reason.
- We discover that Adela had a relationship with Pepe el Romano last year and she was very much in love with him.
- María Josefa manages to get out of her room because she wants to be free, she wants to have children. She carries a lamb which symbolises her desire to nurture a child.

**Key quotation**

**PONCIA. ¡A lo mejor de pronto cae un rayo! A lo mejor, de pronto, un golpe de sangre te para el corazón.**

**BERNARDA. Aquí no pasará nada. Ya estoy alerta contra tus suposiciones.**

*(Act 3)*

## Actividad 13

Traduce las siguientes frases al español. Te ayudarán a comprender lo que ha ocurrido hasta ahora en el tercer acto.

**a)** Prudencia, Bernarda's friend, tells her that she feels sad because her husband does not talk to either his brothers or his own daughter.

**b)** Adela says she would like to spend the night looking at the stars but what she really wants is to spend the night with Pepe el Romano.

**c)** María Josefa escapes from her room and says to Martirio that she would like to go away and have more children.

**d)** Bernarda thinks everything is under control and that nothing can escape her vigilance.

**e)** Adela tells her sister she loves Pepe, and Martirio becomes really angry because she is jealous of her younger sister.

## The final confrontation

Adela decides to open the door and to escape the house to be with Pepe, but Martirio stops her and calls for her their mother. Bernarda and all the others arrive and it is at this moment when Adela is empowered to break Bernarda's stick in two:

> **Key quotation**
>
> (***ADELA arrebata un bastón a su madre y lo parte en dos.***) **Esto hago yo con la vara de la dominadora.**
>
> *(Adela, Act 3)*

She rebels against her mother's authority, but Bernarda takes her gun and shoots at Pepe el Romano, who is lurking outside and has to flee for his life.

At this point, Martirio lies to her sister Adela and, with the intention of hurting her, tells her that Pepe is dead: **'Se acabó Pepe el Romano'** *(Act 3)*. Desperate by what she hears, Adela runs to another room and hangs herself.

Bernarda's reaction is most telling. She declares her daughter a virgin, and wants everyone to know that she died as such. She also forbids all her daughters from crying and tells them that they will have many more years of mourning. Her last word in the play is the same as her first one, a command to all who live in her household, *¡Silencio!*.

The tension builds with Adela's desperation; Timaginas Teatro, 2013

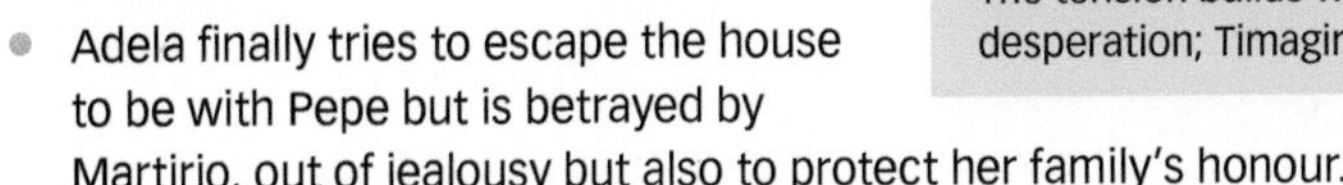

- Adela finally tries to escape the house to be with Pepe but is betrayed by Martirio, out of jealousy but also to protect her family's honour.
- Adela confronts Bernarda and breaks her stick, symbolising her freedom from her mother.
- Bernarda shoots at Pepe, who has to run for his life.
- Adela, thinking that Pepe is dead, commits suicide.
- Even in the moment of her daughter's death, Bernarda's main concern is still for *'el qué dirán'* as she proclaims Adela has died a virgin.

## Actividad 14

Traduce el siguiente resumen del tercer acto al inglés. Te ayudará a entenderlo mejor.

El tercer acto comienza tras las acotaciones del autor que son muy reveladoras ya que las paredes son menos blancas y la acción se desarrolla por la noche. Podemos ver que acaban de terminar de cenar y que una vecina, Prudencia, está con ellas de visita. Hablan de los problemas familiares de Prudencia y sobre la inminente boda de Angustias. Se mencionan los muebles nuevos y sobre todo el anillo de perlas, que simbolizan lágrimas y que nos anticipa el triste final de esta relación.

La trama continúa con más conversaciones entre la familia cuando Prudencia se marcha a rezar el rosario. Angustias les dice que esa noche no vendrá Pepe el Romano porque se va con su madre a la capital. Es un alivio para Bernarda porque así podrá dormir tranquila, es decir, no tendrá que pasar la noche vigilando a su hija, así que Bernarda manda a todas sus hijas a dormir. Cuando Bernarda, Poncia y la Criada se acuestan, vemos salir a Adela, que sabe que Pepe el Romano vendrá esta noche solo para estar con ella, pero Martirio, que ya había oído ruidos y sospechaba de su hermana Adela, la sigue con la intención de impedir que su hermana menor se encuentre con el prometido de Angustias.

Martirio está secretamente enamorada de Pepe y tiene celos de su hermana pequeña. Ella encuentra a Adela, que ha estado con Pepe y que quiere escapar de la casa para vivir con él siendo su amante. Martirio llama a su madre y esta dispara a Pepe con su escopeta. Martirio le dice a Adela que Pepe ha muerto y esta se suicida. Bernarda les prohíbe llorar, proclama que su hija ha muerto virgen – aunque todos sospechamos que eso no es cierto – y termina la obra con la palabra "¡Silencio!".

**Key quotation**

**¡Nos hundiremos todas en un mar de luto! Ella, la hija menor de Bernarda Alba, ha muerto virgen. ¿Me habéis oído? Silencio, silencio he dicho. ¡Silencio!**

*(Bernarda, Act 3)*

## Writing about plot

You need to know the plot (*el argumento/la trama*) very well; but not to simply recount it in an essay question. If you understand the plot you can tackle any question by selecting the relevant information from your knowledge of events and their chronology. Every good answer to any question that could be asked about the play will depend upon this knowledge so make sure you familiarise yourself thoroughly with the text.

## Structure

The play is divided into three acts. Each act corresponds to a part of the classical structure of **a)** exposition **b) rising action** and **c) climax** and **resolution**.

Act 1 introduces the plot and the characters and it establishes the initial conflict: Adela is unhappy about the prospect of being locked in a house for eight years in mourning, hence why she puts on her green dress. Additionally, discovering that her oldest sister Angustias is about to marry Pepe el Romano (Adela's secret love) makes her angry and want to rebel against her mother's authority.

**Key quotation**

**MARTIRIO. ¿Y Adela?**

**MAGDALENA. ¡Ah! Se ha puesto el traje verde que se hizo para estrenar el día de su cumpleaños, se ha ido al corral y ha comenzado a voces: '¡Gallinas, gallinas, miradme!'**
*(Act 1)*

Act 2 is where we see the rising action of the play as the conflict between Bernarda and her **antagonist** Adela starts to become more obvious. The climax and **falling action** happen in Act 3 when Adela confesses her affair with Pepe to Martirio. This act ends with the resolution of the play, when Adela has committed suicide believing that her mother has shot Pepe. Bernarda proclaims her daughter died a virgin and announces more years of mourning.

The structure of the play is cyclical and circular. It is cyclical because each act takes place in a different part of the house, on a different day and at a different time; the action progresses from midday, to afternoon, and then to night through the three acts with a crescendo as the play moves into night.

**rising action** *el nudo* a related series of incidents in a literary plot that build towards the point of greatest interest

**climax** *el clímax* the decisive moment in a plot

**resolution** *el desenlace* the conclusion of the literary plot

**antagonist** *el/la antagonista* a person who actively opposes or is hostile to someone or something

**falling action** *la acción decreciente* the part of a literary plot that occurs after the climax has been reached and the conflict has been resolved

It is circular because each act follows the same pattern: a moment of calm, followed by conflict, ending in a final act of violence. These are elements that help link each act and reinforce the circular structure: the play begins and ends with the same command from Bernarda: *¡Silencio!*. Each of the three acts also begins with the time adverb *'ya'*.

The play begins and ends with death: in Act 1 it is the funeral of Bernarda's latest husband and in Act 3 it is Adela's suicide. There are elements that the audience can see and elements which we only hear about, such as Pepe el Romano, the harvesters, the lynching of the daughter of la Librada. These are some of the conflicts placed to disturb the calm and gradually build tension.

Opposites are continually emphasised in the plot, for example: freedom/oppression, lust/honourable love, house/street, day/night, black/white. The play begins with the **pealing of bells** and ends with Bernarda calling for a new peal of bells in the morning.

**Actividad 15**

La estructura cíclica y circular es una parte importante de la obra. Busca otros ejemplos y citas que ilustren esta estructura.

## The timeline of the play

Lorca mentions the time of day when each of the three acts begins. Act 1 commences at midday, Act 2 at three in the afternoon and Act 3 late in the evening. The time of year is summer, a particularly hot and oppressive one.

We have to take into account that these times cannot realistically belong to the same day. However, with the specific timings of the acts suggesting the progression of a single day, it could be argued that Lorca wanted to create a dual sense of time in the play. Days must realistically pass in between, but the action is presented to us condensed in one **surreal** day (see the later discussion of surrealism on page 39).

- In Act 1, the funeral of Bernarda's husband takes place and we find out that Pepe el Romano wants to marry Angustias, but we do not know yet whether Bernarda approves of this marriage.
- In Act 2, Bernarda has given her approval to this marriage and all the sisters are sewing and preparing the bed linen as part of the trousseau. Martirio has fallen in love with Pepe el Romano – that is why she steals his picture from Angustias' room – and Adela is having an affair with him. All this could not have happened from midday to three in the afternoon of the same day!
- In Act 3, we know that after three days, Pepe will come to the house to formally ask for Angustias' hand in marriage and Adela is already having an illicit relationship with him, sneaking out at night to meet him.

Key quotation

**PONCIA. Oye, Angustias, ¿qué fue lo que te dijo la primera vez que se acercó a tu ventana?**
**ANGUSTIAS. Nada. ¡Qué me iba a decir! Cosas de conversación.**
**MARTIRIO. Verdaderamente es raro que dos personas que no se conocen se vean de pronto en una reja y ya novios.**
*(Act 2)*

**pealing of bells** *el doblar de las campanas* when church bells are rung
**surreal** *surrealista* seemingly unreal

## The timeline within the house

The plot makes the audience feel that things happen slowly. It also makes them experience the repetitive nature of everyday life. The action in the play is slow as there are very few events. The author depicts the dullness of the women's lives very well: their lack of hope, excitement or even a future. They inhabit only the present and are forced to exist in a tedious world inside the house, just as if they were in a prison. Every day is the same for them, sewing and embroidering.

Key quotation

**MARTIRIO. Estoy deseando que llegue noviembre, los días de lluvia, la escarcha; todo lo que no sea este verano interminable.**

**ADELA. Ya pasará y volverá otra vez.**
*(Act 2)*

## The location

The whole play takes place within Bernarda's house, but each act is situated in a different area. Act 1 takes place in a room with very white walls, Act 2 in a white room (less white than the last) and Act 3 in the yard, surrounded by four bluish white walls.

In contrast to the house or the visible space, we have the outside world, embodied by the men, the neighbours, love, happiness, rumours and what in essence is 'alive'. But we also know it is a town without a river, where people have to obtain the water from wells, and this water can be stagnant and poisoned.

Key quotation

**Es así como se tiene que hablar en este maldito pueblo sin río, pueblo de pozos, donde siempre se bebe el agua con el miedo de que esté envenenada.**
*(Bernarda, Act 1)*

## Actividad 16

Céntrate en los lugares donde se desarrolla la obra, dentro y fuera de la casa.

1. Describe la casa con tantos detalles como sea posible, por ejemplo: habitaciones, patios, establos.
2. Describe el pueblo en el que se encuentra la casa.
3. Si puedes, compara tus notas con las de un(a) compañero/a y describe las similitudes y diferencias que puedas encontrar entre la casa de Bernarda y las casas modernas.

Looking at images of the type of place Lorca was writing about can help you visualise the play as you read it

## Actividad 17

Escribe una lista de elementos narrativos que Lorca utiliza en su obra. Puedes incluir: historias de los personajes del pueblo, símbolos, conflictos, ruidos de hombres, cuando Bernarda entra y sale del escenario, etc.

## Writing about structure

It is important to have a clear idea of the structure of the play as this could well relate to many potential essay questions. Remember what you have read about above regarding the cyclical and circular structure. You should learn some appropriate quotations to illustrate this. Also remember the timeline. The events unfold on different days and at different times of the day, although chronologically. Lorca wrote the play with a deliberate structure: it serves a function beyond simply presenting the events of the plot. So consider how its function relates to the rest of the play and its revelation of plot, character and theme.

## Vocabulary

**las acotaciones** stage directions

**el ajuar** trousseau

**la antítesis** antithesis

**el bastón** stick

**bordar** to embroider

**el desenlace** resolution

**el qué dirán** what people will think/say

**el encaje** lace

**la encarcelación** incarceration

**encarcelar** to imprison/incarcerate

**estar asombrado** to be in awe

**la granada** pomegranate

**el hilo** thread

**el látigo** whip

**un lío amoroso** an affair

**el luto** mourning

**la mendiga** beggar

**el muro** wall

**el pozo** well

**recriminar** to blame

**regañar** to tell off

**reprender** to admonish

**los segadores** harvesters

**el sinsabor** trouble, worry

**la yegua** a mare - a female horse or donkey

## Useful phrases

**... es un elemento importante de la trama** ... is an important part of the plot

**el desarrollo de la historia** the unfolding of the plot

**la estructura circular de la obra** the play's circular structure

**Por otra parte, en el siguiente acto...** On the other hand, in the following act...

**El contraste está claro entre...** The contrast is clear between...

**Se puede ver la similitud entre...** One can see the similarity between...

**Como se puede ver al principio/al final de la obra...** As we can see at the beginning/end of the play...

**Los hechos de la obra se desarrollan...** The events of the play take place...

**Descubrimos...** We discover...

**Parece que...** It appears that...

**La acción se centra en...** The plot focuses on...

**En varias ocasiones...** On several occasions...

**A medida que la trama se desarrolla...** As the storyline develops...

**Hacia el final de la obra...** Towards the end of the work...

**Las últimas líneas/páginas nos transmiten un sentimiento de...** The final lines/pages convey a feeling of...

## Biography of Federico García Lorca

Federico García Lorca (1898-1936)

- Federico García Lorca is one of the best-known Spanish writers, and also one of the most loved both in Spain and internationally, for his poetry and his plays.
- He was born in a small village called Fuente Vaqueros in the province of Granada on the 5th June 1898, the oldest of five children of a comfortably-off, middle-class family.
- He studied at the University of Granada where he was a member of a group that included the composer Manuel de Falla. He was passionate about bringing the arts to the people through puppetry (for example, *El maleficio de la mariposa),* which was a popular form of folk art in Spain. He helped organise 'El Concurso del Cante Jondo', a music festival to popularise ***el cante jondo***.
- In 1919, he moved to Madrid where, in the *Residencia de Estudiantes,* he met and became friends with many other writers and intellectuals, including artist Salvador Dalí, poet Rafael Alberti and film director Luís Buñuel. Later on, in Barcelona, he met Margarida Xirgú, a Spanish stage actor and producer who performed in the premiere of *Mariana Pineda* in 1927, and was the first to stage *La casa de Bernarda Alba*, in Buenos Aires in 1945. He also had a clandestine friendship with José Antonio Primo de Rivera, founder of ***La Falange*** and son of General Miguel Primo de Rivera (see Second Republic, page 34).
- In 1931, he formed his own travelling theatre troupe called *La Barraca*, funded by the Republican government with the objective of bringing culture to the people of rural Spain in the form of classical Spanish theatre.
- He was a prolific poet and playwright (his *Obras Completas* is almost 2000 pages in length) and his poetry tackled many different themes such as love, the trials and tribulations of the gypsies, death, Andalusian folklore and personal discovery.
- He has a wide range of styles, for example, sonnets and ballads, of which perhaps the most loved is the 1928 collection known as *El Romancero Gitano*. It comprises 18 **ballads** relating to Andalusian gypsy culture.
- Also important were his ventures into surrealism, the most striking example being *Poeta en Nueva York* which was published **posthumously** in 1940, in which he talked about his homosexuality.

- Of his plays, the most famous are the two rural tragedies, *Bodas de Sangre* (1933) and *Yerma* (1934), and his final work *La casa de Bernarda Alba* (1936), which is sometimes considered to be the third of the series. Lorca called *La casa de Bernarda Alba* a drama rather than a tragedy (see Cultural context, page 40).
- At the age of just 38, Lorca was arrested by the Spanish Civil Guard a matter of weeks after completing *La casa de Bernarda Alba*, at the very start of the Civil War. He was killed for not supporting the new Nationalist regime and for being a homosexual, and was buried in a mass grave.

***el cante jondo*** a traditional vocal style of flamenco music

***La Falange*** Fascist political movement

**ballad** *el romance* a poem or song which tells a story, usually written in short stanzas

**posthumously** *póstumamente* after death

## Tips for assessment

It is useful when studying a literary work to know something of the background of the writer and of the period in which he or she was writing. However, be wary of including this information in an exam essay. References to context must be brief, if used, and only used to support a point you are making about the work itself.

It would be useful for you to find out about the plots of *Bodas de Sangre* and *Yerma* to gain an insight into the recurrent themes of the three plays, as well as the settings and the character relationships in *La casa de Bernarda Alba*.

### Actividad 1

Investiga la vida de Lorca y escribe una lista de los diez momentos más importantes de su vida. Después, si puedes, compara tu lista con la de tus compañeros.

### Actividad 2

Averigua más información sobre la trama, el estilo narrativo (prosa/poesía), los temas, las relaciones, y la ubicación de las obras *Bodas de sangre* y *Yerma.* Ahora, explica cómo te ha ayudado esta información a entender *La casa de Bernarda Alba.*

# Historical and political context

## King Alfonso XIII

Lorca was born in 1898 into a period of political instability in Spain which would last throughout and beyond his lifetime. In this year, Spain lost its overseas empire of Cuba, Puerto Rico and the Philippines to the United States after the Spanish-American war, and in 1899 it sold its Pacific islands to Germany. After a serious economic crisis, the king, Alfonso XIII, decided to support General Miguel Primo de Rivera, who established a **dictatorship** in 1923.

## The Second Republic

In 1927, another economic crisis began and in 1931 the Second Spanish Republic commenced after democratic elections. The king left Spain and went into **exile**.

The Second Republic tried to modernise Spain with a new **constitution** that focused on human rights and the protection of social and personal freedoms. In 1931 it gave women the right to vote. A new flag was designed with the addition of a purple band to differentiate the new regime from the monarchy.

During the Second Republic, the world was suffering an intense economic crisis which lasted into the 1940s. The working and peasant classes were demanding more rights and the country was experiencing a very high level of unemployment. The increasingly tense class divide ended on many occasions in riots, extremist attacks and even social rebellions carried out by **anarchist movements**. The main political parties at the time were the Socialist Party (PSOE), the Socialist Union (UGT) and the Anarchist Union (CNT). **Nationalist parties** in Catalonia and the Basque country also played an important role at this time.

One of the targets of the extremists was the Catholic Church, which still enjoyed many privileges. The extremists burnt churches and killed priests, monks and nuns. These attacks were met with strong opposition from a large part of the mainly Catholic population, who did not agree with these violent methods.

Internationally, the Second Republic suffered from isolation. Many governments would not allow any type of investment in Spain as they feared its **socialist values**.

Lorca therefore lived through, and was writing in, a period of political turbulence, but also a time of exciting new democratic freedoms, **secularisation**, changes to the role of women and class conflict. Not all of these developments were popular: the conservative right-wing (mainly aristocratic) Nationalists led by General Francisco Franco fought the Spanish Civil War of 1936–39 to oppose the move towards democracy.

The flag of the Spanish Second Republic (1931–36)

Following the Nationalist's victory in the war in 1939, many of these freedoms were reversed during General Franco's dictatorship which lasted until 1975.

**Actividad 3**

Busca información sobre la Segunda República (1931–36) y escribe una lista de las nuevas ideas y valores que se introdujeron. En tu opinión, ¿hay evidencia en *La casa de Bernarda Alba* de una tensión entre los nuevos valores republicanos y los tradicionales?

Si puedes, compara tus notas con las de un(a) compañero/a.

## Social context

In this period, many people in Spanish society worked mainly in the **agricultural sector**. Around 50% of Spaniards worked on farms. This is because the **industrial revolution** arrived in Spain later than in other European countries. In certain areas of the country, especially in Lorca's region of the south, there were many landowners *(latifundistas)* who enjoyed greater advantages in life. They owned large expanses of land and they had many people working for them, either farming the land or taking care of the livestock. This can be seen in the play where Bernarda owns land and horses. She has people working for her, like Poncia's sons. These workers were usually illiterate and poor. Many of them would never have the chance to own any land.

**dictatorship** *la dictadura* a country, government, or the form of government in which absolute power is exercised by one person (the dictator)

**exile** *el exilio* person banished or separated from their native land

**constitution** *la constitución* a set of political principles by which a country is governed

**anarchist movement** *el movimiento anarquista* a political movement calling for the end of law and government restraint on society

**Nationalist party** *el Partido Nacionalista* political group advocating or fighting for national independence, a strong national government or federalism (where provinces share power with central government)

**socialist values** *los valores socialistas* left-wing values in which the means of production and distribution of goods are owned and controlled by social groups or by the government, rather than by private business

**secularisation** *la secularización* the removal of religious authority

**agricultural sector** *el sector agrícola* the area of economic activity concerned with cultivating land, raising crops, feeding and raising livestock, and farming

**industrial revolution** *la revolución industrial* the totality of the changes in economic and social organisation that began in about 1760 in England and later in other countries, characterised chiefly by the replacement of hand tools with power-driven machines

As many landowners did not need to exploit all their acreage, some people became itinerant workers, moving from place to place, as the reapers *(los segadores)* in *La casa de Bernarda Alba* do. The rigidity of the class structure meant it was difficult for Spaniards to move from one social class to another. Bernarda exemplifies this when she refused Enrique Humanes permission to court Martirio because of his social class.

**Actividad 4**

Lee atentamente la siguiente cita. ¿Qué nos permite saber de la sociedad española de la época? Considera elementos como el sistema de clases y la sociedad rural. Si puedes, compara tus observaciones con las de un(a) compañero/a.

**Pero yo soy buena perra: ladro cuando me lo dice y muerdo los talones de los que piden limosna cuando ella me azuza; mis hijos trabajan sus tierras y ya están los dos casados...**
*(Poncia, Act 1)*

## Homosexuality during the Second Republic

Part of the social change during the Second Republic was the move to legalise homosexuality. Lorca was homosexual and in 1932 the penal code was changed and homosexuality was no longer categorised as a crime. However, this did not mean that suddenly gay people were openly accepted in society. Homosexuality was often still regarded as morally unacceptable. There were no policies aiming to encourage the integration of gay people into society, unlike the initiatives towards gender equality between men and women. Lorca struggled with the disapproval of homosexuality and never openly acknowledged his sexual orientation. However, much of his work reflects his struggle and repression; he wrote of gay love in his *Sonetos del amor oscuro* and in *La casa de Bernarda Alba* we can interpret a parallel with Lorca's desire to break with the shackles of tradition when Adela wishes to do whatever she wants with her own body: '**¡Mi cuerpo será de quien yo quiera!**' *(Act 2).*

# The role of women

*La casa de Bernarda Alba* is set in Lorca's home region of Andalusia and based on real events he witnessed in his own village, however, the subject matter is not restricted to that area. When he subtitles *it 'Drama de mujeres en los pueblos de España'* he is not suggesting that the life portrayed is typical of women in general; had he wished to say that, he would have written *'Drama de* ***las*** *mujeres en los pueblos de España'*. He specifies *'pueblos'* to differentiate between town and village. (Remember that *pueblo* means village and *ciudad* means town.) The women in the drama do not represent all women in Spain at this time – they are living in an unusual and exaggerated situation.

When Lorca wrote *La casa de Bernarda Alba* in 1936, he focused on the lives of normal people in the villages of Spain. In this play he describes the lives of women, and reflects on their role in society. We can see throughout the play that the role of women is centred within the house. Women were either cleaning, cooking and carrying out domestic work if they belonged to a low social class, like Poncia and the maid (who was also Antonio María Benavides' lover), or sewing and embroidering if they belonged to a higher class like Bernarda's daughters. Having children was also a very important role for women. María Josefa voices the expectation of childbearing as a critical role for women. She chastises Martirio for not having any, and Bernarda for not having allowed her daughters to marry and have children.

**Key quotation**

**Tú eres Martirio, ya te veo. Martirio: cara de martirio. ¿Y cuándo vas a tener un niño? Yo he tenido éste.**

**Ya sé que es una oveja. Pero, ¿por qué una oveja no va a ser un niño? Mejor es tener una oveja que no tener nada. Bernarda, cara de leoparda.**
*(María Josefa, Act 3)*

Traditionally, and even under the Second Republic, in rural areas women had to obey their husbands and did not enjoy economic independence. They lived in their parents' house until they could get married. Living alone, or unmarried but with a man, wouldn't be a decent life; Adela decides to try to take this route out of desperation. Through Adela we can sense the simmering tension of, and desire for change, which reflects the social changes taking place in parts of Spain at the time of the Second Republic. The changing context of repression and freedom in Spanish life is an important theme in the play, demonstrated through all the daughters in different ways as they are all repressed. The only daughter to rebel against the traditionalism that Bernarda represents and perpetuates is Adela.

This is a key element of the play: women are shown to be imprisoned by the stifling traditional values, yet the girls' jailer is not a man, but a woman: their own mother. Women are complicit in maintaining the role of women as home-bound and limited by their own sex. Bernarda implies María Josefa imposed mourning and such limitations on Bernarda as a younger woman: **'Así pasó en casa de mi padre y en casa de mi abuelo.'** *(Act 1)*. Now Bernarda does the same, unquestioningly, and in an increasingly masculine way. She wields a stick for power, she is head of the household; even her name is masculine.

The way **courtship** is depicted is a typical example of how the traditional context is reflected in the play. The formalities surrounding courtship demonstrate a strict morality. Women couldn't spend time with men in bars and at other social events as happens today. They would meet in places like church, where they all attended Mass every Sunday, or when passing by in town. Once the man was interested, he would talk to the woman and then ask the woman's family for permission to talk to her. He would go to the woman's house and, as she was not allowed out, and he not allowed in, talk to her through the windows. Then he would ask for her hand in marriage. This courtship can be seen when Pepe el Romano talks to Angustias through the window and because we know that in three days he will talk to Bernarda to formally ask permission to marry her.

**Key quotation**

**PRUDENCIA. Y Angustias, ¿cuándo se casa?**

**BERNARDA. Vienen a pedirla dentro de tres días.** [...]

**PRUDENCIA (*a* ANGUSTIAS). ¿Te ha regalado ya el anillo?**

**ANGUSTIAS. Mírelo usted. (*Se lo alarga.*)**

**PRUDENCIA. Es precioso. Tres perlas. En mi tiempo las perlas significaban lágrimas.**
*(Act 3)*

**Actividad 5**

Compara las obligaciones y tareas de los diferentes grupos sociales de mujeres en la obra. Considera tanto a las que viven en la casa como a las que son mencionadas en el pueblo. Escribe una lista de tus observaciones sobre el papel de la mujer en esta sociedad. No olvides añadir citas relevantes con cada observación. Si puedes, comparte tus ideas con las de un(a) compañero/a.

# Cultural context

Lorca is one of the most important figures in 20th-century Spanish literature. He belongs to the group of writers known collectively as the Generation of '27, an **avant-garde** movement that included poets such as Rafael Alberti, Vicente Aleixandre, Luis Cernuda and Miguel Hernández. Associated with these writers were representatives of other art forms including the artist Salvador Dalí and the film-maker Luis Buñuel. You will remember some of these names from the biography section. The poets of the Generation of '27 were all already famous when the Civil War broke out in 1936. The war undoubtedly curtailed literary and intellectual progress in Spain, and many of the group suffered death or exile because of their support for the Republicans and the perception of the group as left-wing intellectuals.

## Surrealism

One of the characteristics of the Generation of '27 was their interest and involvement in the new movement known as **surrealism**. In the *Residencia de Estudiantes* in Madrid where Lorca stayed, he met and became friends with Dalí and Buñuel, two key figures in this movement.

He was influenced by this movement in some of his work, in particular in his poetic anthology *Poeta en Nueva York* although be aware that *La casa de Bernarda Alba* is not a work of surrealism. One example of Dalí and Lorca collaborating was in Lorca's play *Mariana Pineda,* about the real-life eponymous woman who having been killed in 1831 as a result of her liberal political leanings, had become part of the folklore of Granada. Dalí created the set design and the costumes. It was during this period that Dalí produced his famous painting *The Persistence of Memory* with its images of 'soft' watches as a symbol of the relativity of space and time.

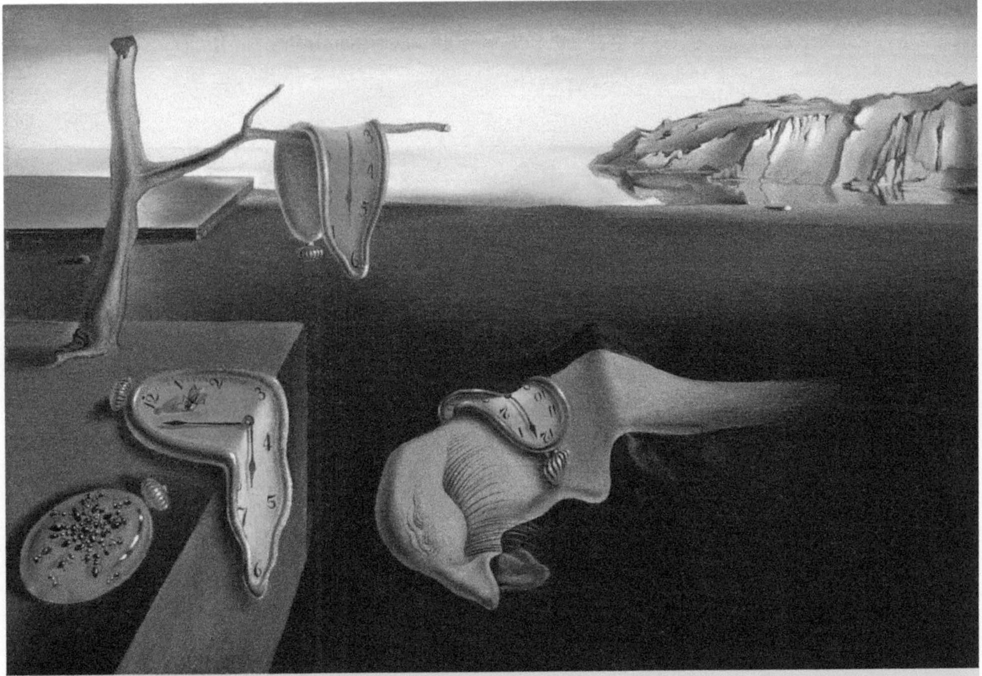

*The Persistence of Memory* by Salvador Dalí, 1931

**courtship** *el cortejo* the act (by one person) of trying to win the favourable attention of another, especially by a man towards a woman

**avant-garde** *vanguardista* new and experimental ideas and methods in art, music, or literature

**surrealism** *el surrealismo* a movement focused on releasing the subconscious mind to find new levels of creativity; often using images and words in unconventional ways

In 1929, Buñuel, in conjunction with Dalí, created his first surrealist silent film, a short work entitled *Un Chien Andalou (An Andalusian Dog).*

The influence of surrealism can be seen in some of Lorca's poetry. For example in '*Ciudad sin sueño*' he writes:

*No duerme nadie por el cielo. Nadie, nadie.*
*No duerme nadie.*
*Las criaturas de la luna huelen y rondan sus cabañas.*

## Folk art

In stark contrast to the modern developments of surrealism, Lorca had a great interest in folklore and traditional tales of Andalusia. The vocal tradition of *cante jondo*, associated with flamenco and the gypsies, influenced his poetry. *Cante jondo* developed from a merging of traditional Spanish music with Indian elements which came with the gypsies.

***El grito***

*La elipse de un grito,*
*va de monte*
*a monte.*
*Desde los olivos,*
*será un arco iris negro*
*sobre la noche azul.*
*¡Ay!*
*Como un arco de viola,*
*el grito ha hecho vibrar*
*largas cuerdas del viento.*
*¡Ay!*
*(Las gentes de las cuevas*
*asoman sus velones)*
*¡Ay!*

In the early 1920s, Lorca's love of *cante jondo*, of puppets and of music in general, brought him close to the composer Manuel de Falla who was living in Granada at the time. The two of them were very involved in the cultural life of the city of Granada and in 1922 were instrumental in the organisation of the first *Concurso de Cante Jondo de Granada*, a celebration of flamenco traditions. They also collaborated on puppet plays and, in 1923, they began writing an operetta, *Lola la comedianta*, but this was left unfinished.

## Cultural origins of the play

Lorca's interest in folklore was certainly an inspiration for his work but so were real events. It may be a surprise to learn that his plot for *La casa de Bernarda Alba* was taken from his own curiosity about, and observations of, a family that lived in the village of Valderrubio where his parents had a house.

As the third of what is known as the 'Rural Trilogy' (*Bodas de sangre*, *Yerma* and *La casa de Bernarda Alba*), *La casa de Bernarda Alba* differs from the other plays in that it is written in prose, but at the same time it can be considered a poetic work with its finely-honed use of language. In all three works, Lorca wished to portray the reality of tragic situations. As the third of the trilogy, *La casa de Bernarda Alba* is the most evolved. *Bodas de sangre*, the first play, is the least realistic as it incorporates more symbolic characters such as the Moon, and the characters are not given names. Poetry plays an important part in the play. *Yerma* contains slightly less poetry but there is still a strong symbolic element, though less pronounced than in *Bodas de sangre*. By the time he wrote *La casa de Bernarda Alba,* Lorca had listened to the critics and took steps to make it more accessible: the balance between reality and symbolism tips more towards reality, with no wholly symbolic characters, no choir, and is mostly written in prose. He uses poetry only for the songs and for speech by María Josefa.

## Actividad 6

Lee este extracto y tradúcelo al inglés con ayuda del vocabulario dado.

**Extraña familia que intrigó al poeta**

... una aldehuela en la que mis padres eran dueños de una propiedad pequeña: Valderrubio. En la casa vecina y colindante a la nuestra vivía "Doña Bernarda", una viuda de muchos años que ejercía una inexorable y tiránica vigilancia sobre sus hijas solteras. Prisioneras privadas de todo albedrío, jamás hablé con ellas; pero las veía pasar como sombras siempre silenciosas y siempre de negro vestidas... había en el confín del patio un pozo sin agua y a él descendía para espiar a esa familia extraña cuyas actitudes enigmáticas me intrigaban. Y pude observarla. Era un infierno mudo y frío en ese sol africano, sepultura de gente viva bajo la férula inflexible de cancerbero oscuro.

**Claude Couffon: *Granada y García Lorca,* page 33. Losada, 1967**

### Vocabulario

**free will** *el albedrío*

**hamlet** *una aldehuela*

**watchdog/guard** *el cancerbero*

**adjoining** *colindante*

**confines** *el confín*

**domination** *la férula*

**mute/silent** *mudo*

**grave/tomb** *la sepultura*

Upgrade

## Writing about context

An awareness of the historical and social context of the play is important in order to understand the life being portrayed. There are cultural aspects of rural life in Spain in the 1930s which need to be understood in order to appreciate the play. For example, make sure you have a basic knowledge of:

- the status of women
- the values and conflicts of the Spanish Second Republic
- the class system and its rigidity
- codes of morality
- agricultural society – lack of education and people farming other people's land.

As a modern audience it can be difficult for us to understand the treatment of women, the supremacy of men and the power of parents. However, it is important to remember the time in which the play was written and its contextual history when making judgements about the characters and the decisions they take. Do not try to impose 21st century attitudes on characters who were not created with modern mindsets. Try to analyse their behaviour by appreciating the viewpoints they demonstrate in the play and the constraints their society may have imposed.

La casa de Bernarda Alba: Being aware of the social and historical context of Lorca's play allows a greater understanding of the themes and characters

## Vocabulary

**el arte folclórico** folk art

**la clase social** social class

**el conflicto** conflict

**el contexto** context

**la crisis económica** economic crisis

**el dictador** dictator

**la discriminación sexual** sex discrimination

**el drama** drama

**el escritor/el autor** writer

**la estructura de clases** class structure

**la Generación del 27** Generation of '27

**el/la gitano/a** gypsy

**la Guerra Civil** Civil War

**la independencia** independence

**la inestabilidad política** political instability

**la poesía** poetry

**el poeta** poet

**la realidad** reality

**la Segunda República** Second Republic

**el simbolismo** symbolism

**el sistema de clases** class system

**el teatro de guiñol** puppetry

**la tragedia** tragedy

**la trilogía** trilogy

**los valores** values

## Useful phrases

**Como se puede ver en el contexto de...** Seen in the context of...

**Se debe tener en cuenta el contexto tradicional de la España rural de la época...** We must consider the context of traditional rural Spain at this time...

**El contexto histórico/social/cultural de la obra nos muestra que...** The historical/social/cultural context of the play illustrates that...

**Teniendo en cuenta el contexto de la Segunda República...** Bearing in mind the context of the Second Republic...

**Los espectadores de la década de 1930 pensarían que...** An audience in the 1930s might consider that...

**Es/era una mujer de su época** She is/was a woman of her time

**Posturas contemporáneas sobre este tema...** Contemporary attitudes towards this subject...

# Characters

*La casa de Bernarda Alba,* as its subtitle clearly suggests, is a 'drama of women in the villages of Spain'. It reflects the life that many women living in rural Spain had to suffer at that time, right before the Civil War: a time of social and political upheaval.

The **protagonists** of the play are all women, who live or work under the **tyranny** of the **matriarch** Bernarda Alba, whose husband has just passed away. In order to better represent their personalities, Lorca gave them names which symbolise their main traits:

**Bernarda**: her name means 'with the strength of a bear'. Her surname, Alba, means 'white' in Spanish, and symbolises her obsession with cleanliness and honour. Her name is also more common as a man's name: Bernardo.

**Angustias**: means 'anxiety' in Spanish; it refers to her age, her ugliness and her desire to marry.

**Magdalena**: her name is associated with love, honesty, fallen women, humility and tears, like Mary Magdalene in the Bible.

**Amelia**: can mean hard-working or sweet and delicate.

**Martirio**: means martyrdom, suffering. It befits a character who suffers from poor health and has a hunchback, and who is also ugly, bitter and jealous.

**Adela**: literally means 'of noble nature'.

**Poncia:** her name is related to Pontius Pilate, who sentenced Jesus to death and then washed his hands of him. She prefers not to get involved with the difficult situations of the house and washes her hands of the issues.

**Prudencia:** means a prudent and sensible character.

**protagonist** *el/la protagonista* the leading character of a drama or other piece of writing

**tyranny** *la tiranía* the use of power that has no limits or bounds; abuse of power

**matriarch** *la matriarca* the female head of a household; an older woman with power or influence in a family

## Classification of characters

The characters of this play can be divided into three categories:

### 1. Visible characters

**Main characters:** These are the characters that can be seen on stage and whose actions have an influence on the plot: Bernarda, Adela, Poncia, Angustias and Martirio.

**Secondary characters:** They only appear briefly in the play or their actions are of little consequence to the plot: María Josefa, Magdalena, the servant, the beggar, Prudencia, Amelia, girl and women 1, 2, 3 and 4.

### 2. Invisible characters

Only Pepe el Romano qualifies for this category. He is never present on stage. The audience only knows what he is doing because of what the other characters say but his actions play a very important part in the plot.

### 3. Characters that are referred to

Like Pepe el Romano they never appear on stage but unlike him they are only mentioned by other characters at a particular time. Their actions play a minor role in the plot. They are: Antonio María Benavides, Enrique Humanes, Paca la Roseta, Adelaida, the woman in the sequins, Don Arturo – the notary, the man with the lace, la Librada's daughter and the harvesters.

### Tips for assessment

Make sure you know which character is which – particularly the five daughters. Find and learn five adjectives to describe each of the major characters to help fix them in your mind.

# Main characters

## Bernarda Alba

Bernarda is the main protagonist of the play. She is the mother of five single daughters. The eldest is Angustias, daughter of her first husband. After the traditional period of mourning, Bernarda remarried and had four more daughters.

### Actividad 1

Empareja las siguientes palabras con su significado en inglés.

| | | | |
|---|---|---|---|
| **1** | dominante | **a** | full of |
| **2** | autoritario/a | **b** | bossy |
| **3** | comportamiento | **c** | blind |
| **4** | egoísta | **d** | with an iron fist |
| **5** | luto | **e** | to conceive |
| **6** | lleno/a de | **f** | domineering |
| **7** | mandón/ona | **g** | authoritarian |
| **8** | ciego/a | **h** | selfish |
| **9** | concebir | **i** | mourning |
| **10** | con mano de hierro | **j** | behaviour |

Bernarda is the eponymous and fearsome central character of the play, played here by Irene Gutiérrez Caba in the 1987 film version directed by Mario Camus

At the beginning of the play, the funeral of Bernarda's second husband, Antonio María Benavides, has just taken place and we learn that she is going to impose an eight-year period of mourning on her daughters, all of whom are of marriageable age, and also on herself. This is the same period of mourning she had for her first husband, which explains the age difference between Angustias and Magdalena. It is likely that Bernarda imposed upon herself the maximum period of mourning of eight years because of her obsession with being better than her neighbours and worrying what people think.

**Key quotation**

**¡Ya sabré enterarme! Si las gentes del pueblo quieren levantar falsos testimonios se encontrarán con mi pedernal. No se hable de este asunto. Hay a veces una ola de fango que levantan los demás para perdernos.** *(Bernarda, Act 2)*

Bernarda is obsessed with '*el qué dirán*' which can be roughly translated as 'what people will say'. In other words, she is constantly mindful of creating the right impression at all costs, be it true or not. We see a prime example of this when Adela dies. What matters the most to Bernarda is Adela's virginal reputation – **'Ella, la hija menor de Bernarda Alba, ha muerto virgen'** *(Act 3)* – although all indications are that this was not the case.

Bernarda follows the traditional Spanish code of honour with all its hypocrisy. This code demands that women cannot have premarital sex, even though men can. Women are not allowed to move out of their parents' house until they marry, women have to work in the house, and they are not equal to men.

**Key quotation**

**Aquí se hace lo que yo mando. Ya no puedes ir con el cuento a tu padre. Hilo y aguja para las hembras. Látigo y mula para el varón. Eso tiene la gente que nace con posibles.**
*(Bernarda, Act 1)*

Bernarda is a terribly proud person who makes decisions without caring about their impact. We can see this when she decides to impose the eight years of mourning, irrespective of the needs and wishes of her daughters, who are all of marriageable age. This will be the catalyst of the drama. She is in fact incarcerating her daughters, as they will not be allowed to leave the house during the mourning period: **'En ocho años que dure el luto no ha de entrar en esta casa el viento de la calle'** *(Act 1).*

Even Angustias, who is not the deceased's daughter, has to participate in the mourning before getting married, although she does not have to wait for eight years to marry.

Bernarda considers herself and her family to be of a wealthier class, superior to those around her, whom she treats with disdain. Speaking of the maid (la Criada) she says, **'Los pobres son como los animales; parece como si estuvieran hechos de otras sustancias'** *(Act 1).* Bernarda wants nothing to do with her neighbours, only to maintain a **façade** to impress them. She is scared of their possible gossip, questioning Poncia to know what they might be saying about her: **'¿Siguen diciendo todavía la mala letanía de esta casa?'** *(Act 3).*

## Actividad 2

Escribe un sinónimo y un antónimo de las siguientes palabras.

| | | | | |
|---|---|---|---|---|
| **a)** dominante | **b)** luto | **c)** egoísta | **d)** autoridad | **e)** rebeldía |
| **f)** prisión | **g)** fuerte | **h)** tradicional | **i)** desesperado | **j)** irracional |

Bernarda is **omnipresent** in the play. Even when she is not in the same room as the other members of her household they talk about her or measure their actions according to her possible reaction. For example, when Poncia (her long-serving housekeeper) is making sure everything is clean, she fears Bernarda's wrath: **'Si Bernarda no ve relucientes las cosas me arrancará los pocos pelos que me quedan'** *(Act 1).* Her character comes through clearly and unequivocally as a domineering and dictatorial person.

**façade** *la fachada* a deceptive outward appearance; also the main front/face of a house

**omnipresent** *omnipresente* constantly present

**Key quotation**

¡Mandona! ¡Dominanta!

Tirana de todos los que la rodean. Es capaz de sentarse encima de tu corazón y ver cómo te mueres durante un año sin que se le cierre esa sonrisa fría ...
*(Poncia, Act 1)*

Bernarda's first and last words in the play are *¡Silencio!*. She wants everyone in her household to obey in silence. This is reinforced with the use of her stick, which she sometimes hits on the floor when she gives a command, as a symbol of her authority and power.

Bernarda will resort to violence to control those around her and uses her stick on three occasions to do so: once against Angustias for wearing make-up; then against Martirio for answering back; and once against Adela, when she finds out that she has been with Pepe el Romano. On the third occasion, Adela rebels and breaks the stick. Bernarda often reacts with aggressive behaviour, physically knocking the fan which Adela offers her away because it is not black *(Act 1)*. She even attempts to kill Pepe el Romano by firing a shot at him, in order to preserve the honour of her family.

Bernarda is cruel and insensitive towards those who live in her house. She did not allow her daughter Martirio to marry Enrique Humanes despite the fact that this may have been her only offer of marriage. Bernarda is also cruel in her treatment of her mother María Josefa, who is senile. She is not allowed to leave the house and is kept locked away. This example also illustrates *'el qué dirán'*: Bernarda would not want her neighbours to witness her mother's dementia and erratic behaviour.

In summary, it can be said that Bernarda displays traits more frequently associated with men, at a time when Spain was a patriarchal society. She disciplines her daughters and staff, defends the house against perceived danger, and oversees the financial affairs of the household such as the breeding of horses. She is also confrontational when addressing everyday issues.

**Key quotation**

BERNARDA (*en voz baja, como un rugido*). ¡Abre, porque echaré abajo la puerta!

*Pausa. Todo queda en silencio.*

¡Adela! (*Se retira de la puerta.*) ¡Trae un martillo!
*(Act 3)*

PRUDENCIA. Has sabido acrecentar tu ganado.
*(Act 3)*

## Actividad 3

1. Rellena los huecos con la palabra apropiada de la lista de abajo. ¡Cuidado, sobran varias palabras!

   Bernarda es un personaje [1]______________, casi inhumano. Fue concebido por Lorca como una mujer fuerte, [2]______________ y [3]______________. No solo es capaz de gobernar una casa llena de mujeres en edad de [4]______________ con mano de hierro, sino que se permite ignorar las [5]______________ de Poncia con respecto al comportamiento de sus hijas, que comienzan a actuar de manera casi irracional y [6]______________, como si estuvieran en una [7]______________, después de la imposición de los ocho años de [8]______________. Bernarda representa la [9]______________ ciega, la tradición más [10]______________ y el completo desdén por los deseos vitales de los individuos.

| | | | | |
|---|---|---|---|---|
| **a)** mandona | **b)** cruel | **c)** prisión | **d)** desesperada | **e)** positivo |
| **f)** advertencias | **g)** habladora | **h)** autoridad | **i)** tirana | **j)** rebeldía |
| **k)** luto | **l)** sociedad | **m)** historias | **n)** casarse | **o)** autoritario |

2. Usa la primera parte de esta actividad como punto de referencia para escribir una descripción más detallada de Bernarda. Busca y utiliza tus propias citas para justificar tus opiniones.

### Tips for assessment

In your exam, you will have to present points of view about characters, using evidence from the text to support your points. Remember to consider, as relevant to the question you are answering, the following aspects: physical description, accessories, personality traits, relationships and symbols. For example, a description of Bernarda would feel incomplete without reference to the stick, her black clothes, and her authoritative manner.

## Adela

Although Lorca considered *La casa de Bernarda Alba* to be a drama, not a tragedy, it could be said that Adela is a tragic heroine. She is tragic in that she dies unnecessarily, taking her own life because she is maliciously led to believe, by her sister Martirio, that her lover is dead. She is a heroine because she is the only one in Bernarda Alba's family who is prepared to stand up to the oppressive tyranny with which the household is ruled. However, she does not meet all the criteria for a tragic heroine: she does not experience a moment of recognition when she realises that she has in error, or by flaw of character set herself upon a course that will destroy herself and others. On the contrary, her death is the result of an error on her part.

The youngest and the best looking of Bernarda's daughters, it is 20-year-old Adela who rebels against her mother's tyranny. The fact that she is consumed with desire for Pepe (and that this is reciprocated as far as we know) is the cause of the tragic ending to the drama. We understand from Poncia that her feelings for Pepe are not new:

Adela tries to escape the tyranny of Bernarda Alba

**Key quotation**

PONCIA. No es toda la culpa de Pepe el Romano. Es verdad que el año pasado anduvo detrás de Adela, y ésta estaba loca por él, pero ella debió estarse en su sitio y no provocarlo. Un hombre es un hombre.

CRIADA. Hay quien cree que habló muchas noches con Adela.

PONCIA. Es verdad. *(En voz baja.)* Y otras cosas.
*(Act 3)*

We can assume that being the youngest daughter, she would not have been allowed to be the first to marry. Daughters typically married in order of age.

Her rebellion is also against the archaic morality that pervades the play and that is sustained by her mother and the villagers who live around them.

She tells Martirio that Pepe wants her to live with him and she contravenes all the accepted codes of conduct by engaging in a sexual relationship with him. Furthermore, we come to believe that she is pregnant, particularly when we see her reaction to the call to kill the daughter of la Librada who has an illegitimate child.

From the beginning of Act 1, we see her rebelliousness; she carries a red and green fan rather than the more appropriate black one for mourning; she puts on her green dress; she complains about the imposition of the very long period of mourning which she sees as robbing her of her youth: '... este luto me ha cogido en la peor época de mi vida para pasarlo' *(Act 1).* The green and red are a splash of colour in otherwise monochromatic surroundings which represent passion and sensuality and are our first indication of Adela's desire to cut herself free. The culmination of her rebellion comes when she breaks her mother's stick in two, the stick being the symbol of tyranny in the house.

Adela is a character with vitality and a joy of life. She also has a sense of humour which appears to be lacking in the other characters:

**'MAGDALENA. ¿Y las gallinas qué te han dicho?**
**ADELA. Regalarme unas cuantas pulgas que me han acribillado las piernas. (*Ríen*)'** *(Act 1)*.

Adela is passionate and has an independence of spirit which contradicts everything that Bernarda expects from her daughters. She challenges established morality openly, telling Poncia **'Mi cuerpo será de quien yo quiera'** *(Act 2)* and even defiantly intimates to her mother that she has had a sexual relationship with Pepe: **'Yo soy su mujer'** *(Act 3)*.

**Key quotation**

**Ya no aguanto el horror de estos techos después de haber probado el sabor de su boca. Seré lo que él quiera que sea. Todo el pueblo contra mí, quemándome con sus dedos de lumbre, perseguida por los que dicen que son decentes, y me pondré delante de todos la corona de espinas que tienen las que son queridas de algún hombre casado.**
*(Adela, Act 3)*

## Tips for assessment

If you are writing about a character such as Adela, you can use quotations not only to support your assertions about her character and behaviour, but also to comment on her as a wider representation of women. If Lorca is making a wider comment about the role of women in Spanish society at the time he wrote the play, what might he be using Adela to say?

**Actividad 4**

1. Toma notas sobre los siguientes puntos relacionados con el personaje de Adela e ilústralas con citas apropiadas.
   - **a)** El amor y el cortejo con Pepe el Romano
   - **b)** ¿Cuáles eran sus obligaciones en casa?
   - **c)** ¿Cómo pasaba su tiempo libre? – ¡Aparte de obsesionarse día y noche con Pepe el Romano!
   - **d)** Incluye una descripción de sus gustos, vestuario, accesorios, de su apariencia física, etc.
2. Para entender mejor al personaje de Adela escribe un párrafo sobre cómo interactúa con los otros habitantes de la casa.

## Poncia

Poncia is the same age as Bernarda. They have known each other all their lives and Poncia has worked for Bernarda for many years. She is a widow and used to be married to Evaristo el Colorín, which was his nickname because he bred a bird called a linnet (*un colorín*). It is worth noting that Poncia calls Bernarda by the familiar *'tú'*, which even her own daughters don't. Although there is a mutual dependency and Poncia is a confidante for Bernarda, their views differ and there is no affection in the relationship.

At the start of Act 1, Poncia plays an important role in providing the audience with information about Bernarda. It is she who tells us that her employer is '**¡Mandona! ¡Dominanta! [...] Tirana de todos los que la rodean**' *(Act 1).*

She is perceptive and knows everything that goes on in the house. She warns Bernarda, although her advice and warnings fall on deaf ears. Her interventions are frequent, but not necessarily for good reasons; rather, they enable her to stir up anxiety in Bernarda. In fact, Poncia dislikes Bernarda and is scornful of her daughters:

**Key quotation**

**... pero un día me hartaré [...] Ese día me encerraré con ella en un cuarto y le estaré escupiendo un año entero: 'Bernarda, por esto, por aquello, por lo otro', hasta ponerla como un lagarto machacado por los niños, que es lo que es ella y toda su parentela.**
*(Poncia, Act 1)*

Bernarda always treats Poncia as the servant she is, reminding her of her station in life:

'**PONCIA. Contigo no se puede hablar. ¿Tenemos o no tenemos confianza?**
**BERNARDO. No tenemos. Me sirves y te pago. ¡Nada más!**' *(Act 1).*

She also reminds her that she knows the truth about her background:

'**BERNARDA. El lupanar se queda para alguna mujer ya difunta ...**
**PONCIA. ¡Bernarda, respeta la memoria de mi madre!**
**BERNARDA: ¡No me persigas tú con tus malos pensamientos!**' *(Act 2).*

Poncia is sarcastic about Bernarda: '**Ella la más aseada, ella la más decente, ella la más alta. Buen descanso ganó su pobre marido**' *(Act 1).* She is not averse to stealing from her employer and encourages the maid to do so too: '**Le he abierto la orza de chorizas [...] Entra y llévate también un puñado de garbanzos. ¡Hoy no se dará cuenta!**' *(Act 1).*

In her relationship with Bernarda's daughters, she is the antithesis of their mother, happy to speak with them in risqué language and talk about sexual matters: '**Entonces Evaristo se acercó, se acercó que se quería meter por los hierros, y dijo con voz muy baja: '¡Ven, que te tiente!''** *(Act 2).* She takes vicarious pleasure in recounting the sexual exploits of others, for example her account of the episode concerning Paca la Roseta, or the arrival of the prostitute and the fact that she had paid for her own son to take advantage of such a woman.

**Key quotation**

**Claro es que no le envidio la vida. Le quedan cinco mujeres, cinco hijas feas, que quitando a Angustias, la mayor, que es la hija del primer marido y tiene dineros, las demás mucha puntilla bordada, muchas camisas de hilo, pero pan y uvas por toda herencia.**
*(Poncia, Act 1)*

**Actividad 5**

1. Considera la mutua dependencia que existe entre Bernarda y Poncia. ¿Crees que podrían sobrevivir la una sin la otra?
2. En tu opinión, ¿crees que a la Poncia le importa realmente alguna de los habitantes de la casa? ¿Tiene alguna favorita?
3. Escribe un párrafo explicando por qué Lorca incluyó este personaje en la obra. ¿Se podría decir que cumple la función de la conciencia de Bernarda? Justifica tu respuesta con citas y explicaciones.

Angustias is submissive to Bernarda but cruel to her sisters; Timaginas Teatro, 2013

## Angustias

Angustias is Bernarda's eldest and the only daughter of Bernarda's first husband, who remains unnamed throughout the play. She is also the heir to a considerable fortune, which is the reason why Pepe el Romano wants to marry her, despite the fact that she is older and not very attractive.

Angustias is aware that it is better to be wealthy than attractive, and she reminds her less wealthy sisters of this.

**Key quotation**

**ANGUSTIAS. Afortunadamente pronto voy a salir de este infierno.**

**MAGDALENA. ¡A lo mejor no sales!**

**MARTIRIO. ¡Dejar esa conversación!**

**ANGUSTIAS. Y, además, ¡más vale onza en el arca que ojos negros en la cara!**
*(Act 2)*

As the eldest she is also the one who is most under the influence of Bernarda. Her mother attacks her and reduces her to tears for wearing make-up in Act 1. She has her own doubts about Pepe, and she confides them to her mother in Act 3. Angustias also does not feel happy about marrying him, suggesting that for her it is more important to marry to escape Bernarda's tyranny than for love.

**Actividad 6**

Empareja estos adjetivos que describen a Angustias.

| | | | |
|---|---|---|---|
| **1** | fea | **a** | proud |
| **2** | adinerada | **b** | insecure |
| **3** | enfermiza | **c** | supercilious |
| **4** | orgullosa | **d** | unforgiving |
| **5** | dócil | **e** | diffident |
| **6** | altiva | **f** | old |
| **7** | apocada | **g** | wealthy |
| **8** | insegura | **h** | obedient |
| **9** | despiadada | **i** | sickly |
| **10** | mayor | **j** | ugly |

Her relationship with her sisters is tense. They envy her for different reasons. She is going to marry one of the most attractive men in town, she is going to be the first one to leave the house and they envy her wealth. They talk behind her back and criticise her for her many faults. Martirio steals her picture of Pepe, and Adela has an affair with him.

**Key quotation**

**... Lo natural sería que te pretendiera a ti, Amelia, o a nuestra Adela, que tiene veinte años, pero no que venga a buscar lo más oscuro de esta casa, a una mujer que como su padre habla con la nariz.**
*(Magdalena, Act 1)*

Poncia describes her as being too old to marry and thinks she would not survive giving birth to her first child.

She is also given an engagement ring with three pearls instead of diamonds by Pepe el Romano: pearls mean tears and therefore this is not a good omen for the future wedding.

## Actividad 7

Rellena los huecos con las palabras apropiadas del recuadro de abajo.

Angustias, la hija [1]__________ de Bernarda Alba, ha [2]__________ una gran fortuna de su padre, que fue el [3]__________ marido de Bernarda. Eso quiere decir que las otras cuatro hijas solo son sus medio hermanas.
Ellas [4]__________ su dinero y piensan que es fea y está [5]__________.
Angustias [6]__________ casarse con Pepe para [7]__________ de la casa de su madre. Su [8]__________ le ha comprado un anillo de tres [9]__________ que simbolizan [10]__________.

| | | | |
|---|---|---|---|
| **a)** lágrimas | **b)** novio | **c)** primer | **d)** enfermiza |
| **e)** perlas | **f)** heredado | **g)** mayor | **h)** escapar |
| **i)** desea | **j)** envidian | | |

Angustias is submissive to her mother but is cruel towards her siblings. She regularly reminds them that she will soon be married and away from the house and shows them her engagement ring telling them what her fiancé has said to her.

**Key quotation**

**ANGUSTIAS. Pues nada: 'Ya sabes que ando detrás de ti, necesito una mujer buena, modosa, y esa eres tú, si me das la conformidad.'**

**AMELIA. ¡A mí me da vergüenza de esas cosas!**
*(Act 2)*

Martirio is the most bitter of Bernarda's daughters; Estudio Corazza, 2014

## Martirio

Martirio is the fourth daughter of Bernarda Alba. She is described as being ugly and ill, with a hunchback. She seems aware of her faults and describes herself as having a well of poison within her. She is pessimistic, repressed by her mother and the morals of the time. She had the chance of marrying a man, Enrique Humanes, but Bernarda never allowed this union as she considered him of an inferior class. This makes Martirio suffer and behave like a **martyr**. It has also poisoned her relationship with her mother, who demonstrates their mutual antipathy when she hits her and calls her names in Act 2.

**martyr** *el mártir* someone who deliberately invites or exaggerates suffering to gain sympathy; someone who suffers and dies for their faith

**Key quotations**

**BERNARDA** *(avanzando y golpeándola con el bastón).* **¡Mala puñalada te den, mosca muerta! ¡Sembradura de vidrios!**
**MARTIRIO** *(fiera).* **¡No me pegue usted, madre!**
**BERNARDA. ¡Todo lo que quiera!**
**MARTIRIO. ¡Si yo la dejo! ¿Lo oye? ¡Retírese usted!**
*(Act 2)*

**MARTIRIO. Es preferible no ver a un hombre nunca [...] Dios me ha hecho débil y fea y los ha apartado definitivamente de mí.**
*(Act 1)*

## Actividad 8

Empareja las palabras que describen a Martirio.

| | | | |
|---|---|---|---|
| **1** | envidiosa | **a** | bitter |
| **2** | fea | **b** | observant |
| **3** | jorobada | **c** | jealous |
| **4** | observadora | **d** | hunchbacked |
| **5** | amargada | **e** | ugly |

Martirio is very jealous of Angustias because her wedding has been approved by Bernarda, unlike her own aspirations of a relationship with Enrique Humanes. She is a traditional character who accepts the oppression by her mother even if she does not like it, but it makes her ill and extremely unhappy. This is another reason why she will not tolerate others escaping the morality and rules of the time. If she suffers, she feels others should also suffer and have to abide by the same rules, including her own younger sister, Adela, telling her in Act 2, **¡Que pague lo que debe!**

Martirio is also jealous of her younger sister, Adela. We know that at some point her relationship with her was different and that she loved her very much, just like Poncia says. However, her jealousy and her passion for Pepe el Romano blind her and she tells Adela that she does not regard her as a sister anymore but as a woman. Martirio warns her sister in Act 2 that she would not tolerate her illicit relationship with Pepe:

**Key quotation**

**PONCIA. ¡Adela, que es tu hermana, y además la que más te quiere!**

**ADELA. Me sigue a todos lados. A veces se asoma a mi cuarto para ver si duermo. No me deja respirar. Y siempre: ¡Qué lástima de cara! ¡Qué lástima de cuerpo, que no va a ser para nadie!**

*(Act 2)*

## Actividad 9

Rellena los huecos con la palabra apropiada del recuadro de abajo.

Martirio es otra de las hijas de Bernarda Alba. Es un personaje muy [1]__________ que siente [2]__________ de Angustias, porque se va a casar [3]__________ que ella nunca se casó por [4]__________ de su madre, que rechazó a su pretendiente, Enrique Humanes. También tiene [5]__________ de su hermana menor, Adela. Martirio está [6]__________ enamorada de Pepe, y es por esa razón por la que le [7]__________ la foto de Pepe a Angustias. [8]__________ a su envidia, no permite que Adela vaya con Pepe y [9]__________ a toda la casa al final del acto tercero. Por último, miente y le dice a su hermana Adela que Pepe ha [10]__________ después del disparo de Bernarda. Como consecuencia de esta mentira Adela se suicida.

| | | | |
|---|---|---|---|
| **a)** roba | **b)** culpa | **c)** muerto | **d)** alerta |
| **e)** debido | **f)** celos | **g)** envidia | **h)** negativo |
| **i)** secretamente | **j)** mientras | | |

Her jealousy turns into hatred and at the end of the play she intentionally hurts Adela by telling her that Bernarda has killed Pepe el Romano. When her sister asks why she has said something that horrible, she replies saying she would do anything to hurt her. Even after her death she is jealous; she thinks Adela was the most fortunate of them all as she had the chance to be with a man, unlike her.

**Key quotations**

**PONCIA. ¿Pero lo habéis matado?**
**MARTIRIO. ¡No! ¡Salió corriendo en la jaca! [...]**
**¡Por ella! Hubiera volcado un río de sangre sobre su cabeza. [...]**

**MARTIRIO. Dichosa ella mil veces que lo pudo tener.**

*(Act 3)*

## Pepe el Romano

As an invisible character Pepe el Romano is never seen on stage and never says a word, but like Bernarda he is omnipresent in the play through the other characters' dialogue. It is difficult to decide whether he is a main or a secondary character. He does not have any lines but his actions are key for the development of the plot. Without Pepe el Romano there would never have been a drama in the house of Bernarda Alba.

He is described as being young and the most handsome man in the town. At 25 years old he is much younger than his fiancée Angustias, who is 39 years old. We assume that he belongs to a suitable family as Bernarda would not have allowed their relationship, considering her obsession with honour and reputation.

**Key quotations**

**ADELA.** ¿Por eso ha salido detrás del duelo y estuvo mirando por el portón? *(Pausa.)* Y ese hombre es capaz de...
**MAGDALENA.** Es capaz de todo.
*(Act 1)*

**MAGDALENA.** Y un hombre tan guapo.
**ANGUSTIAS.** ¡No tiene mal tipo!
*(Act 2)*

**Actividad 10**

Encuentra un sinónimo de estos adjetivos que describen a Pepe el Romano.

| guapo | joven | amante | mentiroso | egoísta |
|---|---|---|---|---|
| seductor | omnipresente | atrevido | libre | viril |

Pepe's personality is never described by any of the characters but we can infer it through his actions. He is a greedy man who wants to have access to Angustias' wealth through marriage and everyone except for Bernarda and Angustias seems to have this opinion.

**Key quotation**

Si viniera por el tipo de Angustias, por Angustias como mujer, yo me alegraría, pero viene por el dinero. Aunque Angustias es nuestra hermana aquí estamos en familia y reconocemos que está vieja, enfermiza...
*(Magdalena, Act 1)*

Pepe started having a relationship with Adela, Angustias' younger sister, a year before he decided to court his **betrothed**. We presume that he loves Adela – he certainly feels a deep sexual attraction for her – but not enough to marry her or not more than he loves Angustias' money.

Pepe is the **catalyst** for the climax in the play. He is able to seduce three of Bernarda's daughters:

1. Angustias: he wants to marry her because of her inheritance.
2. Adela: he is having a secret love affair with her.
3. Martirio: who loves him in silence.

**betrothed** *el/la prometido/a* someone who is engaged to marry

**catalyst** *el catalizador* a person or thing that brings about change

The feelings that he awakens within these three women will create tension, jealousy and hatred and a terrible conflict that will end in disaster. Pepe also represents a dangerous threat to Bernarda's authority and morality to the point that she attempts to murder him when she finds out that he is seeing Adela in secret.

**Key quotation**

**BERNARDA. Angustias tiene que casarse en seguida.**
**PONCIA. Claro, hay que retirarla de aquí.**
**BERNARDA. No a ella. ¡A él!**
**PONCIA. Claro, ¡a él hay que alejarlo de aquí! Piensas bien.**
*(Act 2)*

# Minor characters

## Magdalena

At 30 years old, Magdalena is the second oldest of Bernarda's daughters and the oldest of the four girls fathered by her second husband, Antonio María Benavides. We learn in the opening scene that she loved her father most and that she faints during the funeral Mass. We understand too that she was the favourite of her father. Bernarda says to her, **'Ya no puedes ir con el cuento a tu padre'** *(Act 1).* She cries easily and suffers the wrath of her mother for this: **'Magdalena, no llores. Si quieres llorar te metes debajo de la cama'** *(Act 1).*

Her name originates from Mary Magdalene and she is portrayed as a sad woman; having looked around her grandmother's room where she saw their childhood pictures she reflects: **'Aquélla era una época más alegre'** *(Act 1).*

When Amelia mentions to her that her shoelace is undone and she could fall, Magdalena's response is: '¡Qué más da! [...] ¡Una menos!' *(Act 1)* which means she does not care if she falls and breaks her neck, she has nothing to look forward to. She is resigned to respecting the authority of her mother and indeed shares her views to some degree on class and the role of women:

**Key quotations**

Malditas sean las mujeres.
*(Magdalena, Act 1)*

¡Cada clase tiene que hacer lo suyo!
*(Magdalena, Act 2)*

However, at the same time she shows admiration for Adela's determination to stand up against it and she wants her to be happy: '¡Pobrecilla! Es la más joven de nosotras y tiene ilusión. ¡Daría algo por verla feliz!' *(Act 1)*. Magdalena is convinced that she herself will never marry: 'Sé que yo no me voy a casar. Prefiero llevar sacos al molino' *(Act 1)*.

Although she is a calmer character than her sisters and occasionally even shows kindness, Magdalena still harbours a lot of bitterness towards Angustias who is to marry Pepe and thus escape the house. They frequently bicker, for example at the beginning of Act 2:

'ANGUSTIAS. Afortunadamente pronto voy a salir de este infierno.
MAGDALENA. ¡A lo mejor no sales!' *(Act 2)*.

She says later that she will do no sewing for any child of Angustias: 'Yo no pienso dar una puntada' *(Act 2)*.

## Amelia

Amelia is the third daughter of Bernarda and is 27 years old. She only plays a minor role in the play. She is shy and has a caring personality. She believes that marriage should only happen because of love; she also thinks that being born a woman is the worst type of punishment as they have to abide by so many rules, but being a man is different as they are allowed to do so many things: 'Nacer mujer es el mayor castigo' *(Act 2)*.

Amelia is very **naïve** regarding men and is also very inexperienced. This can be observed in her comments about Angustias' courtship and when she hears what happened to Adelaida: 'Ya no sabe una si es mejor tener novio o no' *(Act 1)*.

**naïve** *un/una ingenuo/a* a person showing a lack of experience, wisdom, or judgement; gullible

When Amelia talks to her sisters it is usually to make an everyday comment like **'¿Has tomado la medicina?'** *(Act 1)* or to participate in a conversation with her sisters, sometimes echoing what one has just said, such as **'Es verdad. Daba miedo. ¡Parecía una aparición!'** *(Act 3)*. She maintains a cordial relationship with them, however we can assume she is also jealous of Angustias when she says, **'Yo también. Angustias tiene buenas condiciones'** *(Act 1)*.

Amelia can be associated with resignation because she accepts the imposition of the period of mourning imposed by Bernarda and accepts what life brings to her. Amelia is Martirio's closest confidant and Martirio nearly tells her of her suspicions about why Adela is always tired during the day when Amelia is about to leave the stage in Act 2.

## María Josefa

Bernarda's mother, María Josefa, is 80 years old and is suffering from senile dementia. Because of Bernarda's fear of *'el qué dirán'* she is kept locked away out of sight, only to appear on stage on two occasions when she has escaped from her incarceration. On these rare but poignant appearances there is, mixed with her ramblings, a perception and clarity of thought regarding the events of the household.

**Key quotations**

**No quiero ver a estas mujeres solteras, rabiando por la boda, haciéndose polvo el corazón...**
*(María Josefa, Act 1)*

**Pepe el Romano es un gigante. Todas lo queréis. Pero él os va a devorar, porque vosotras sois granos de trigo...**
*(María Josefa, Act 3)*

María Josefa's longings for marriage and children echo those of her granddaughters and we know that what is impossible for the 80 year old will also be an unfulfilled dream for the younger women.

Through her treatment of her mother, we learn more about the hard-hearted Bernarda. Kept locked away from the sight of neighbours, María Josefa would otherwise be a cause of shame to Bernarda. When María Josefa escapes and Bernarda tells the maid to take her out into the yard but to keep her away from the well, it is not for María Josefa's protection, but to keep her out of view of the neighbours:

**'BERNARDA. Ve con ella y ten cuidado que no se acerque al pozo.**
**CRIADA. No tengas miedo que se tire.**
**BERNARDA. No es por eso. Pero desde aquel sitio las vecinas pueden verla desde la ventana'** *(Act 1)*.

There is clearly no affection between mother and daughter, and nor is there a significant relationship between María Josefa and her granddaughters, who tend to find her behaviour amusing rather than sad.

At the end of Act 1, they all conspire together to drag the old woman back into her 'prison'; an even more restricting one than that endured by the daughters. However, there is a hint that María Josefa herself behaved in the same way as Bernarda when her husband died because when Bernarda is telling her daughters about the eight years of mourning, she says: **'En ocho años que dure el luto no ha de entrar en esta casa el viento de la calle. Haceros cuenta que hemos tapiado con ladrillos puertas y ventanas. Así pasó en casa de mi padre y en casa de mi abuelo'** *(Act 1).*

In this way, Lorca reveals her character not to be as simple as it might first appear: perhaps she was also regarded as tyrannical when she imposed the period of mourning on Bernarda as a younger woman. It reinforces the idea that the customs the family follow are traditional, and the suffering of women is something which has always been endured, and is also continued by the women themselves.

## La Criada

We never find out the name of the servant, perhaps to emphasise that she belongs to a lower class. She belongs to the lowest class in Bernarda's house and is also under the authority of Poncia. She shares Poncia's opinion of Bernarda and her daughters and Poncia feels free to criticise Bernarda to her, calling her *mandona* and *dominanta* in front of her. She is very submissive and never rebels against Bernarda's authority unlike Poncia who argues with Bernarda about the nature of the problem in the house. The servant only complains to Poncia that Bernarda never gives her any time to rest: **'Bernarda no me deja descanso en todo el día'** *(Act 3).*

La Criada is submissive but despises Bernarda; Timaginas Teatro, 2013

At the beginning of Act 1 we find out that she misses Bernarda's late husband, Antonio María Benavides, as she had an affair with him. She is also crying for him and screams to herself that she will miss him.

**Key quotation**

***(rompiendo a gritar)*. ¡Ay Antonio María Benavides, que ya no verás estas paredes, ni comerás el pan de esta casa! Yo fui la que más te quiso de las que te sirvieron. *(Tirándose del cabello.)* ¿Y he de vivir yo después de haberte marchado? ¿Y he de vivir?**
*(Criada, Act 1)*

The servant is the character used by Lorca to describe social classes in the play. Bernarda even says that poor people are like animals, or that they are made of a different stuff: **'Los pobres son como los animales. Parece como si estuvieran hechos de otras sustancias'** *(Act 1).*

Interestingly, the servant shows no mercy towards the beggar who comes to the house looking for the food scraps, and instead she behaves towards her like Bernarda would have behaved towards the servant herself. She tells the beggar that she would keep the scraps for herself. In this dialogue we also find out how poor the servant is, who lives in a hut with an earthen floor. The author uses their conversation to present the idea that repression leads to more repression: **'Por la puerta se va a la calle. Las sobras de hoy son para mí'** *(Act 1).*

The servant carries out the hard work in the house. She feels confident talking to Poncia and to Bernarda's daughters but she is terrified of Bernarda. The servant is also the person who takes care of María Josefa.

## Prudencia

Prudencia is a minor character, who only appears at the beginning of Act 3. She is Bernarda's neighbour and, as her name suggests, she is prudent and seems to be the opposite of Bernarda. Where Bernarda is the head of the family, Prudencia is controlled by her husband. She is suffering family problems and does not know what to do.

Prudencia is a traditional person who complies with what is socially acceptable, although unlike Bernarda she is unhappy about her situation. However, because she accepts her circumstances, she is the ideal friend for Bernarda. Prudencia is not aware of the domestic problems happening at Bernarda's house and this becomes apparent when she asks about the future wedding. We know her husband has fought with his brothers about an inheritance and also with his daughter. Bernarda shows her intolerance when she agrees with Prudencia's husband: **'Es un verdadero hombre'** *(Act 3).* She is a devout Catholic as we can infer when she asks about the last pealing of bells for the rosary, and says that she finds church her only solace.

**Key quotation**

**Yo dejo que el agua corra. No me queda más consuelo que refugiarme en la iglesia, pero como estoy quedando sin vista tendré que dejar de venir para que no jueguen con una los chiquillos.**
*(Prudencia, Act 3)*

## Mendiga

The beggar woman plays a very small role in the play but nonetheless one with some significance. Her treatment by the maid illustrates clearly how behavioural traits are transmitted: the maid is treated badly by her mistress so she now gives similar treatment to the only person below her in the social pecking order: **'Por la puerta se va a la calle. Las sobras de hoy son para mí'** *(Act 1).*

We know that on this particular day, the maid does not have to make do with scraps because she has been able to steal from the larder, so her treatment of the beggar seems unnecessarily cruel.

## Enrique Humanes

A character only referred to in passing, Enrique Humanes was the potential suitor of Martirio. He did not turn up at her window on the agreed night and subsequently married someone richer. This relationship had been thwarted by Bernarda who had sent him a message telling him not to keep the appointment at Martirio's window that night. Her justification was his lower status: **'¡Mi sangre no se junta con la de los Humanes mientras yo viva! Su padre fue gañán'** *(Act 2).*

### Writing about characters

Upgrade

It is not uncommon for there to be exam questions based around character studies. It is therefore vital that you analyse the characters of the play and do not overlook the unseen ones whose role is very important. They are inextricably linked with the themes of the play. You need to know what the characters represent; why they act and react as they do in the play; how they interact with each other and why.

## Vocabulary

**amargo** bitter

**la aventura** affair (romantic)

**celoso/envidioso** jealous

**los colorines** linnets

**corregir** to correct

**criticar** to criticise

**espantoso** fearsome

**el esposo/el marido** husband

**el funeral/el entierro** funeral/burial

**la herencia** inheritance

**las hijas** daughters

**invisible** invisible

**mandona** domineering

**la mayor** oldest

**la menor** youngest

**el periodo de luto/de duelo** period of mourning

**los personajes visibles** visible characters

**pesimista** pessimistic

**rasgos personales** personal traits

**rebelde** rebellious

**senil** senile

**la tensión/el conflicto** tension

**tirana** tyrant

**el veneno** poison

**la violencia** violence

## Useful phrases

**Esta disparidad entre Bernarda y Adela nos muestra que...** This contrast between Bernarda and Adela illustrates...

**Es un personaje dócil/sumiso** She is a submissive/accepting character

**Tiene una personalidad violenta/abusiva** She has a violent/abusive personality

**Puede ser descrita como...** She can be characterised as...

**Poncia la describe como...** Poncia describes her as...

**El personaje sirve como/de...** The character serves as a...

**Sus acciones nos muestran que...** His/Her actions show us that...

**Si la examinamos con más detenimiento...** If we examine her more closely...

**Desde un punto de vista moral** From a moral point of view

**Desde una perspectiva psicológica** From a psychological perspective

**Este personaje juega un papel imprescindible en...** This character plays a vital role in...

# Language

Lorca demonstrates a complete mastery of dialogue in *La casa de Bernarda Alba*. Each character uses expressions corresponding to their social class and the interactions are short and lively; this makes the play feel very real. This feeling is enhanced by the use of a particular stylistic technique that Lorca called '*poetización del lenguaje cotidiano*' which can be translated as 'expressing everyday language through poetry'. This technique gives the characters a more pronounced sensibility – Lorca uses everyday language, such as popular expressions, as he would use poetry.

In *La casa de Bernarda Alba* there are popular expressions that help to set the scene in a rural environment, but they also reflect Lorca's knowledge of popular language.

## Actividad 1

Hay una amplia gama de refranes que enriquecen el tono rural de la obra. ¿Pero qué significan en inglés? Traduce las siguientes expresiones.

| Expresión popular | Meaning in English |
|---|---|
| Lengua de cuchillo | |
| Mal dolor de clavo le pinche en los ojos | |
| Gori-gori | |
| Cae el sol como plomo | |
| La noche quiere compaña | |

## Actividad 2

Empareja las expresiones del texto con su explicación y en cada caso identifica quién habla.

| | | | |
|---|---|---|---|
| **1** | Es capaz de sentarse encima de tu corazón *(Act 1)* | **a** | No le importa verte sufrir |
| **2** | Por un oído me entra y por otro me sale *(Act 2)* | **b** | Hay una falta de hombres elegibles |
| **3** | Yo no me meto en los corazones *(Act 3)* | **c** | No me interesa |
| **4** | A mí las cosas de tejas arriba no me importan nada *(Act 3)* | **d** | Lo que pasa en otro lugar es el asunto de otros |
| **5** | Porque no hay carne donde morder *(Act 3)* | **e** | No decido acerca de los sentimientos de otra persona |

# Symbolism

## Water

Water has its very own meaning within the play and becomes a poetic element. To begin with there is water in the description of the village as a *pueblo de pozos* whose stagnant water can be poisoned and is always drunk with fear. Later, the well evolves as the place that María Josefa is not allowed to go for fear of being seen by her neighbours.

In the second act, Martirio yearns for the arrival of the rain **'que llegue noviembre, los días de lluvia, la escarcha; todo lo que no sea este verano interminable'**, which symbolises the end of the summer, the heat and the end of the aggravation in the house. Later, Poncia uses an analogy of the river **('¡No llegará la sangre al río!')** to suggest that the daughters won't act on their words. She then uses the sea to describe Bernarda's refusal to face problems which are right in front of her: **'Cuando una no puede con el mar lo más fácil es volver las espaldas para no verlo'** *(Act 3)*.

There are many more examples where the symbol of water is used to convey different meanings: sometimes death, as is the case for stagnant, disease-carrying water; sometimes freedom, e.g. the rain; and sometimes sexual desire as when Adela says, **'Voy a beber agua'** *(Act 3),* i.e. she wants to quench her lust and **'Me despertó la sed'** *(Act 3)*.

**Actividad 3**

Busca más representaciones en la obra del agua como símbolo. Escribe una frase explicando cada uno de los que encuentres.

The changing colour of the set is an important reflection of the narrative, seen in this production which relocates the story to rural Iran, Almeida Theatre London, 2012

## The house

The stage directions offer a practical description of the house – its layout and its furnishings. They also convey the symbolism of the changing light, as the walls become less white in each act, signifying the approaching doom.

The house where all of the action happens represents something more than just a dwelling; it represents a prison where nothing escapes Bernarda's eye: **'En esta casa no hay un sí ni un no. Mi vigilancia lo puede todo'** *(Act 3)* and Poncia likens it to a war zone: **'esta casa de guerra'** *(Act 3)*.

The façade of the house also serves as a double meaning for the deceptive façade which Bernarda shows to her neighbours. She hides inside the house behind a self-righteous front that everything is alright within.

The house's thick walls repress its inhabitants, while at the same time they interact with them. This symbolic meaning becomes apparent when the white stallion is kicking the walls in Act 3 because it wants to be free. The stallion also represents sexual desire which, in this case, is being repressed by the girls' confinement in the house.

**Key quotation**

*Se oye otra vez el golpe.*
PONCIA. ¡Por Dios!
PRUDENCIA. ¡Me ha retemblado dentro del pecho!
BERNARDA. [...] pero dejadlo libre, no sea que nos eche abajo las paredes. *(Se dirige a la mesa y se sienta otra vez.)*
*(Act 3)*

**Upgrade**

## Tips for assessment

Make sure you know the layout of Bernarda Alba's house, where the action takes place, and the significance of the changes of location within each act.

## The stick

*El bastón* symbolises tyranny and authoritarianism. It can also be taken to represent masculinity. Bernarda, who has taken over the 'male role' in the house, is rarely seen without it and it frequently features in the stage directions:

**Key quotations**

*(dando un golpe de bastón en el suelo)*
*(Act 1)*

*(avanzando con el bastón)*
*(Act 1)*

*(Sale lentamente apoyada en el bastón)*
*(Act 1)*

*(avanzando y golpeándola con el bastón)*
*(Act 2)*

*(... da un golpe en el suelo)*
*(Act 2)*

*(ADELA arrebata un bastón a su madre y lo parte en dos)*
*(Act 3)*

Adela breaks Bernarda's stick, the symbol of her authority

Bernarda uses the stick when she is punishing, or chastising her daughters, for example when she chastises Angustias for looking at the men or Martirio for stealing the photo of Pepe. At other times she uses it for its rightful purpose as a support to lean on.

The stick is therefore a symbol of authority and the breaking of it by Adela in Act 3 is the moment of greatest overt rebellion against this authority. This is in theory the end of Bernarda's domination: the triumph of liberty over oppression. It is fleeting, however, as Adela commits suicide shortly afterwards.

## Colour

### Black and white

As mentioned in the section on Plot, Lorca's intention was to create a photographic documentary in *La casa de Bernarda Alba.* Photographs in Lorca's time were still predominantly taken using black-and-white film. The use of these two colours, black and white, is relevant throughout the play.

The colour white represents many things, such as purity and virginity. It also represents Bernarda's obsession with cleanliness and with '*el qué dirán*':

**Key quotation**

**Limpia bien todo. Si Bernarda no ve relucientes las cosas me arrancará los pocos pelos que me quedan.**
*(Poncia, Act 1)*

Through María Josefa, Lorca also associates this colour with sex in reference to sea foam: '**¿Por qué aquí no hay espuma?**' *(Act 3)* and with childhood, as she is holding a lamb when she escapes in the third act. The characters' underwear is white, which is all that Adela is wearing at the end of the third act when she has been with Pepe el Romano.

Black retains its common meaning: death and sadness as the colour of mourning – all the women have to wear this colour. Even their fans have to be black. Black is also the colour of night, and it is during the night when bad things happen in Lorquian theatre. Adela's death happens in the third act, and we know because of her conversation with Bernarda that it is a particularly dark night.

**Key quotation**

**AMELIA. ¡Qué noche más oscura!**
**ADELA. No se ve a dos pasos de distancia.**
**MARTIRIO. Una buena noche para ladrones, para el que necesite escondrijo.**
[...]
**ADELA. Tiene el cielo unas estrellas como puños.**
*(Act 3)*

### Green

The colour green represents rebellion, sexual desire and death in this play and in Lorca's poetry. All these elements are expressed in Adela's green dress. She wears it because she does not want to be locked in the house for eight years, she wants to go out and be free. She wants to be with Pepe el Romano but we also know what happens to her in the end: her rebellion is the cause of her death. The sexual and passionate representation also occurs in the colours of Adela's fan that she offers her mother in Act 1. Its red flowers represent passion and its green ones her desire for freedom. The symbolism of this simple item, a fan, is striking against the monochrome of the scene.

The association of the colour green with sex occurs again when the young reaper with green eyes organises the visit to the olive grove with the prostitute. **'... quince de ellos la contrataron para llevársela al olivar... El que la contrataba era un muchacho de ojos verdes, apretado como una gavilla de trigo'** *(Act 2).*

**Key quotation**

**¡Ah! Se ha puesto el traje verde que se hizo para estrenar el día de su cumpleaños, se ha ido al corral y ha comenzado a voces: "¡Gallinas, gallinas, miradme!" ¡Me he tenido que reír!**
*(Magdalena, Act 1)*

Another interpretation of the colour green is as a symbol for death. It is no coincidence that the only character who wears green at some point in the play is the only one who dies. This symbol occurs frequently in Lorca's poems and one of the best-known examples is 'Romance sonámbulo'. Here is a short extract:

***Romance sonámbulo***

*Verde que te quiero verde.*
*Verde viento. Verdes ramas.*
*El barco sobre la mar*
*y el caballo en la montaña.*
*Con la sombra en la cintura*
*ella sueña en su baranda,*
*verde carne, pelo verde, ...*

**Actividad 4**

Haz una lista de todos los colores que utiliza Lorca en *La casa de Bernarda Alba* y escribe con tus propias palabras en español cuál es su significado. No te olvides de utilizar las citas apropiadas.

## The stallion

*El caballo garañón* represents virility, masculinity, and specifically Pepe el Romano. It also represents sexual desire. In Act 2, when Amelia and Martirio are discussing hearing noises in the stable yard at night, Amelia says: **'Quizá una mulilla sin desbravar'**. Martirio mutters her response: **'Eso, ¡eso!, una mulilla sin desbravar'** – in this double entendre she is likening Adela to the unbroken mule.

When the stallion is kicking the walls, Bernarda gives instructions for him to be let out into the yard, whereas the female horses are to be kept inside.

**Key quotation**

**Pues encerrad las potras en la cuadra, pero dejadlo libre, no sea que nos eche abajo las paredes.**
*(Act 3)*

Here we have a parallel: men are to be let free, lest they bring down the walls; women (the daughters of Bernarda) are to be restrained in the confines of the house.

The night is very dark and here the image of the ghostly stallion predicts death:

**Key quotation**

**MARTIRIO. Una buena noche para ladrones, para el que necesite escondrijo.**
**ADELA. El caballo garañón estaba en el centro del corral. ¡Blanco! Doble de grande, llenando todo lo oscuro.**
**AMELIA. Es verdad. Daba miedo. ¡Parecía una aparición!**
*(Act 3)*

**Actividad 5**

Ya hemos hablado del caballo garañón, pero este no es el único caballo de la obra – aparte de las yeguas. Nos referimos al caballo de Pepe el Romano. ¿Hasta qué punto comparte el caballo de Pepe el mismo significado simbólico que el caballo garañón?

Lorca also uses other animals as images. Bernarda is likened to a lizard, a symbol of repression; here Poncia fantasises about bringing that repression to an end: **'hasta ponerla como un lagarto machacado por los niños'** *(Act 1)* and also: **'¡Vieja lagarta recocida!'** *(Mujer 1, Act 1).*

In Act 3, María Josefa is positioned in stark contrast with Bernarda who brandishes a stick; María Josefa enters carrying a lamb, a substitute child. As noted in her character analysis, she is obsessed with having more children (see page 62). As María Josefa recites her poetic message she refers to Bernarda as having the face of a leopard. A leopard can symbolise the need for privacy and watchfulness over one's surroundings – an image which is well-suited to Bernarda.

She refers to Magdalena as "*cara de hiena*", the hyena: an animal that feeds off weak prey. María Josefa is in all likelihood referring to the numerous occasions on which Magdalena has spoken cruelly and maliciously about her sisters – in particular, about Angustias.

# Natural elements

Lorca uses various natural elements to enrich the language used by his characters.

## The heat and trees

The play takes place during a particularly hot summer, and there are several references to the heat. For example, Martirio can't wait for November and Magdalena asks Poncia to open the door in an attempt to get a draught of air into the room where they are sewing. This heat reinforces the feeling of oppression as nobody can leave the house to seek cooler air. It is also a symbol of sexual desire – when Adela is arguing with Martirio she mentions the heat inside of her.

The heat is a symbol of freedom. The harvesters work in August in extreme heat and Adela says she would like to be a reaper so she could come and go whenever she wanted: **'Me gustaría segar para ir y venir'** *(Act 2).* The harvesters are poetically compared to burnt trees, also reinforcing this meaning of freedom and also of virility. The trees represent life in constant evolution and the fact that they are burnt shows intensity of desire. This meaning is reinforced in the reapers' song, full of sexual innuendos:

**"Abrir puertas y ventanas**
**las que vivís en el pueblo;**
**el segador pide rosas**
**para adornar su sombrero."**
*(Act 2)*

As explained below, flowers *(rosas)* symbolise women, and the reapers are asking for women.

**Key quotations**

**PONCIA. De muy lejos. Vinieron de los montes. ¡Alegres! ¡Como árboles quemados!**
*(Act 2)*

**AMELIA. ¡Y no les importa el calor!**
**MARTIRIO. Siegan entre llamaradas.**
*(Act 2)*

## The stars and flowers

Adela mentions the stars and how she enjoys watching shooting stars because they represent change. The stars mean hope, especially for Adela who is in a very difficult situation with Pepe. She wishes for things to change, referring to the morals that oppress her: **'A mí me gusta ver correr lleno de lumbre lo que está quieto y quieto años enteros'** *(Act 3).*

The flowers represent women and love. For example, Paca la Roseta came back from her affair with a crown made of flowers, the harvesters ask for flowers in their song, referring to women, and María Josefa is wearing flowers on her head and on her chest when she declares she wants to marry again and have more children.

**Key quotation**

**PONCIA. Lo que tenía que pasar. Volvieron casi de día. Paca la Roseta traía el pelo suelto y una corona de flores en la cabeza.**

***(Se oyen unas voces y entra en escena MARÍA JOSEFA, la madre de BERNARDA, viejísima, ataviada con flores en la cabeza y en el pecho.)***

*(Act 1)*

The fan that Adela offers to her mother, which Bernarda rejects violently and throws on the floor, is decorated with red and green flowers. Lorca is already warning the audience of things to come as Bernarda is rejecting not only the fan, but Adela's hopes for love and freedom.

**Key quotation**

**ADELA. Tome usted. *(Le da un abanico redondo con flores rojas y verdes.)***

**BERNARDA *(arrojando el abanico al suelo)*. ¿Es éste el abanico que se da a una viuda? Dame uno negro y aprende a respetar el luto de tu padre.**

*(Act 1)*

## Pearls

In many cultures, pearls are considered to be unlucky, a symbol of tears, and for this reason they are not usually chosen as gems for an engagement ring. However, the ring given to Angustias by Pepe comprises three pearls:

**'PRUDENCIA. Es precioso. Tres perlas. En mi tiempo las perlas significaban lágrimas.**

**ANGUSTIAS. Pero ya las cosas han cambiado'** *(Act 3).*

Although Angustias argues that things have changed, Adela corrects her: **'Yo creo que no. Las cosas significan siempre lo mismo. Los anillos de pedida deben ser de diamantes'** *(Act 3).*

## Actividad 6

Lee el artículo 'Los símbolos de una generación' con detenimiento.

### Los símbolos de una generación

El famoso poeta y dramaturgo Federico García Lorca utilizó una amplia gama de símbolos en su drama *La casa de Bernarda Alba* para crear un bello e inolvidable lenguaje, usando prosa poética, para transmitir sus ideas e inquietudes.

El símbolo del agua lo usa de forma magistral para transmitir tanto la represión como el deseo de libertad y de anhelo sexual. ¿No es extraordinario como un mismo elemento puede representar ideas tan opuestas? Desde el mar que menciona María Josefa, pasando por la sangre que vertería Martirio y sin olvidar el pozo de la casa de Bernarda, ese pozo al que María Josefa no le está permitido acercarse por culpa del maldito qué dirán, ese qué dirán que será el último culpable de la muerte de Adela.

Pero no solo es el agua, es la misma naturaleza la que hace acto de presencia en la pluma de Lorca, las estrellas que tanto admira Adela, el caballo blanco que quiere echar la casa abajo para ser libre y para poder montar a las potras y qué decir de esos hombres quemados como árboles que trabajan entre llamaradas de fuego. No puedo dejar de pensar en qué símbolos habría usado para contar otras historias si no hubiera tenido tan trágico final a tan temprana edad.

Después de haber leído el texto, decide si las siguientes frases son Verdaderas (V), Falsas (F) o No mencionadas (N).

**a)** El famoso escritor usó una limitada variedad de símbolos en su obra.

**b)** Lorca fue capaz de expresar lo que quería gracias al uso de los símbolos.

**c)** El dramaturgo usa muchos símbolos, pero ninguno es tan completo como el agua.

**d)** Bernarda maltrata a María Josefa por culpa de *el qué dirán.*

**e)** El caballo es un símbolo de sexualidad y de fortaleza.

**f)** La naturaleza es una gran fuente de símbolos.

**g)** La luz de las estrellas simboliza la inteligencia de Adela.

**h)** Los segadores no se consideran símbolos de la naturaleza.

**i)** El fuego representa el calor del verano, no es la fuente de luz de los trabajadores del campo.

**j)** El escritor del artículo quiere saber más de Lorca.

**Actividad 7**

Traduce el segundo párrafo de la actividad 6 al inglés (*'El símbolo del agua ... la muerte de Adela'*).

## Photographic documentary

Lorca points out at the beginning of the play that it is intended as a photographic documentary. The symbolism of black and white is examined above, but the following section will further explore this unusual description.

There is a famous quotation from Lorca that helps us to understand his conception of theatre, which he used in 1936 when he was talking about *La casa de Bernarda Alba.* His explanation helps us to understand the behaviour of his characters in the play.

*El teatro es la poesía que se levanta del libro y se hace humana. Y al hacerse, habla y grita, llora y se desespera. El teatro necesita que los personajes que aparezcan en escena lleven un traje de poesía y al mismo tiempo que se les vean los huesos, la sangre.*

Theatre is poetry that gets out of a book and becomes human. And when this happens, it (poetry) speaks and screams, cries and becomes desperate. Theatre needs the characters that come to stage to wear a suit made of poetry and at the same time to show that they are made of flesh and blood.

Photographic documentary contains a tension between simply capturing reality and creating a work of art. The author is making a connection between writing and photography, as both types of artistic expression enable an artist to capture moments and elements of their environment no matter how brief and short-lived. Also, most photographs at the time were in black and white, just as in the text these are the two main colours; the black of mourning and the white of the walls and of the girls' trousseaus. This approach means *La casa de Bernarda Alba is* not a realistic play, but a **stylised** representation of a drama that happened in Andalusia. For example, Andalusia is full of colour, yet here it appears in black and white.

Just as the writing is often poetic, so the visual aspect of the staging is also clearly artistic. The reality described by Lorca has two elements: life inside the house which could be described as a prison, a convent and repressive; and life outside the house, which represents freedom, sexuality, men and immorality. Lorca's reality is therefore poetic. The symbolism discussed above and his characters are stylised.

The other word, 'documentary', refers to how the play describes life within Bernarda's house. Lorca's intention of creating a photographic documentary makes this play different in style to the other two plays in the trilogy (*Bodas de sangre* and *Yerma*).

**stylised** *estilizado* presented in a non-realistic way

Unlike the other two plays, in *La casa de Bernarda Alba* he uses very little poetry, music and chorus. He also abandons the use of **oneiric** elements and gives real names to his characters, names which are full of symbolism but which were common names at the time.

In his photographic documentary, the author is able to explore the reality of his time, where there are social classes, and criticise this social system. But the play is able to become something bigger that goes beyond a particular moment in time. Lorca has created a play that can describe many realities and that is relevant nowadays as it embraces universal themes such as repression, desire for freedom, jealousy and love.

**oneiric** *onírico* relating to dreams

The idea of the play as a photographic image is often used in promotional material; in this case for the 1987 film version

**Key quotation**

***Habitación blanca del interior de la casa de BERNARDA. Las puertas de la izquierda dan a los dormitorios. Las hijas de BERNARDA están sentadas en sillas bajas, cosiendo. MAGDALENA borda. Con ellas está la PONCIA.***
*(Act 2)*

## Actividad 8

Escribe un párrafo en español de no más de 90 palabras resumiendo lo que has entendido del artículo '¿Fotografía o teatro?'. Puedes incluir:

- La importancia de los colores blanco y negro. *(cuatro detalles)*
- Cómo consigue Lorca que la obra se parezca a un documental fotográfico. *(tres detalles)*

**¿Fotografía o teatro?**

Gracias a su maestría del lenguaje, Federico García Lorca escribe una obra de teatro que logra parecerse a un documental fotográfico en blanco y negro.

Puede parecer sorprendente a primera vista que pueda existir alguna similitud entre el teatro y la fotografía, pero es cuando nos centramos en la cromática imperante en la obra cuando ocurre el milagro. El blanco y el negro permean y contrastan entre sí en toda la obra, empezando por las paredes blancas de la casa, el blanco de las sábanas que tienen que coser y bordar, así como las enaguas blancas que las hijas de Bernarda llevan por la noche y el caballo garañón. El negro viene de la mano del luto decretado por Bernarda y la noche cerrada del tercer acto.

Pero Lorca se sirve de otra herramienta para crear esta sensación. Con el uso de las acotaciones cada acto comienza como si fuera una fotografía de la vida diaria de esta familia tan inusual y conforme transcurre la acción parece como si cada una de estas fotografías cobraran vida y fueran lentamente contándonos lo que ocurre dentro de la casa. Porque hay que tener en cuenta que la trama se desarrolla lenta pero inexorablemente, como una ola de mar que va cogiendo fuerza hasta que se estrella contra la orilla.

# Figures of speech

*La casa de Bernarda Alba* is written in prose except for two short songs and the poetry used by María Josefa. Even so, there is a poetic quality throughout with the frequent and sustained use of symbols (discussed above) and other figures of speech, which are not all what could be classed as 'realistic' in terms of everyday Andalusian language.

In the first stage direction, Lorca describes the silence permeating the set as 'shadowy' – **'Un gran silencio umbroso se extiende por la escena'**. Silence cannot be shadowy, but this metaphor is an evocative phrase which clearly shows that this silence is oppressive.

Lorca frequently uses colloquialisms with the intention of making the play accessible to the people of his time. Some examples can be seen in the insults (*pérfida*), curses **'Treinta años lavando sus sábanas [...] ¡maldita sea!'** *(Poncia, Act 1)* and threats **'De aquí no sales con tu cuerpo en triunfo'** *(Act 3)* which are used. He also makes use of slang such as *'endemoniadas'* used predominantly by the lower-class characters.

As the play opens, the conversation between Poncia and la Criada, realistic to a degree, contains various figures of speech and colloquialisms. When Poncia suggests to la Criada that she take **'un puñado de garbanzos'** *(Act 1),* she is using a colloquial expression which refers not to chickpeas specifically, but to a quantity of food in general.

Later, she describes Bernarda as capable of **'sentarse encima de tu corazón'** *(Act 1)*, meaning that she has the means to make a person suffer. Poncia likens herself to a faithful dog, submissive to Bernarda's needs and demands: **'Pero yo soy buena perra; ladro cuando me lo dice y muerdo los talones de los que piden limosna cuando ella me azuza…'** *(Act 1)*.

Lorca also uses the local dialect of Andalusia (*andalucismos)* because he was from Granada. An example of this includes Bernarda's insult to Martirio in Act 2 after she is caught out for having taken Pepe's photograph: **'¡Mala puñalada te den, mosca muerta!'** and Magdalena's insinuation: **'siempre cabeza con cabeza pero sin desahogarse con nadie'**.

La Criada uses the image **'sangre en las manos'** *(Act 1)* to convey the idea of an excessive amount of work. It does not mean literally that her hands are bleeding.

In Act 2, Poncia refers to the suffocating heat as **'fuego de la tierra'**. Later, when she tries to explain to Bernarda that the daughters are suffering, she says, **'Tus hijas están y viven como metidas en alacenas. Pero ni tú ni nadie puede vigilar por el interior de los pechos'** *(Act 3)*. She means that they are imprisoned as if shut in a wardrobe, but in spite of that no one, not even Bernarda, can control what goes on in their hearts.

Bernarda, on the other hand, responds: **'Mis hijas tienen la respiración tranquila'** *(Act 3)*, meaning that her daughters have no cause for agitation.

When Bernarda says that there are no grounds for gossip, she uses the expression **'Porque no hay carne donde morder'** *(Act 3)*.

There are further references to the stifling atmosphere of the house – Angustias says: **'Afortunadamente pronto voy a salir de este infierno'** *(Act 2)* – this hell.

**Actividad 9**

1. Encuentra frases en las que la casa es descrita o comparada con una prisión.
2. Haz una lista de algunas de las figuras retóricas utilizadas por las hijas de Bernarda.

## Writing about language

Although on one level the language of *La casa de Bernarda Alba* appears to be straightforward prose and to some degree colloquial, it is in fact poetic prose. There is an abundance of imagery and symbolic language with which you need to familiarise yourself, and be able to explain. For example, why is poetic imagery used at certain points? How do different characters use language in different ways, and what is the effect of this? How does Lorca use language to reflect the context of the play, and what does his choice of imagery reveal about the play's themes?

You also need to understand how Lorca successfully created the semblance of a 'photographic documentary', taking realistic elements of rural Andalusian life but altering them to create a stylised drama. There are layers of meaning in Lorca's use of language which you need to explore to enable you to answer exam questions thoroughly.

## Vocabulary

**el abanico** fan

**el aislamiento** confinement

**la autoridad** authority

**el caballo garañón** stallion

**la cárcel** prison

**desbravar** to break in, tame

**el deseo sexual** sexual desire

**el dialecto** dialect

**el documental fotográfico** photographic documentary

**los elementos naturales** natural elements

**estallar** to break (out)

**estilizado** stylised

**las estrellas fugaces** shooting stars

**las expresiones populares** popular expressions

**familiar/coloquial** colloquial

**las flores** flowers

**los insultos** insults

**la libertad** freedom

**la lluvia** rain

**la luz cambiante** changing light

**masculino** masculine

**la muerte** death

**la opresión** oppression

**la ovejita/el cordero** lamb

**las perlas** pearls

**la pureza** purity

**la rebelión** rebellion

**la represión** repression

**el símbolo** symbol

**la tiranía** tyranny

## Useful phrases

**Habla de forma agresiva** She has an aggressive way of speaking

**Examinemos el estilo del dramaturgo** Let us examine the playwright's style

**El caballo garañón simboliza...** The stallion serves to symbolise...

**es altamente simbólico** is highly symbolic

**Lorca usa un lenguaje poético** Lorca uses poetic language

**el uso de figuras retóricas, tales como...** the use of figures of speech, such as...

**Su personalidad/estado de ánimo la/lo expresa a través de su forma de hablar** Her personality/mood is expressed in her choice of words

**Una cita breve puede mostrar que...** A short quotation can show that...

## Authority and freedom

The code of mourning permeates every part of the girls' lives, even how they dress

The main themes in *La casa de Bernarda Alba* are the repression caused by a strict and authoritative moral code and the desire for freedom expressed by the very people who suffer this tyranny. It is the confrontation between two different attitudes to life and therefore, two different ways of seeing the world. One is strict and inflexible and the other one is open and forward-thinking.

Bernarda represents authority; she embodies the importance of reputation, social convention and tradition. She uses this moral code as justification for imposing her will on everyone living under her roof. Her influence is tyrannical and repressive.

On the other hand, there are those who want freedom and who will fight for it. Their main aspiration in life is freedom and this is represented by two very different characters: Adela and María Josefa.

The conflict is introduced in the play from the very beginning. Bernarda denies her daughters and her own mother the freedom to decide on what they want to do with their lives, and enforces repressive rules on them as head of the family. For example, she 'commands' the eight-year period of mourning: **'Aquí se hace lo que yo mando...'** *(Act 1).*

Everyone living in Bernarda's house has to follow these rules. It could be argued that they have been enslaved by her will and by her lack of empathy. The one who objects the most is Adela, the youngest of Bernarda's daughters, who does not want to lose her beauty locked in the house: **'no quiero perder mi blancura'** *(Act 1).* The rest of the daughters accept Bernarda's decision with different degrees of resignation. María Josefa is locked in her room and is not allowed to go anywhere unsupervised. She is the one who suffers the most restrictions in the house.

Bernarda's authoritative attitude is described in the first conversation between Poncia and la Criada. Therefore, when Bernarda makes her first appearance on stage, the audience already have an opinion of her and this is quickly confirmed when she demands silence.

The title of the play conveys the meaning of this authority. It is Bernarda's house; she is the head of this home and it belongs to her. Bernarda is the owner of the house but also of the people who live there. The word 'house' in the play has a poetic meaning and it describes the inside world (prison) as opposed to the outside world (freedom).

This repressive attitude stems from Bernarda's obsession with honour and with keeping up appearances, as befits a person with pretensions of higher status than others in the village. Bernarda's dictatorship wants to preserve the honour of her house: **'Yo no me meto en los corazones, pero quiero buena fachada y armonía familiar'** *(Act 3)*. Her behaviour is intended to maintain her reputation as well as her daughters', but her actions mean her house becomes a prison or a white tomb.

Bernarda dictates acceptable behaviour for her daughters in relation to men and she does not accept disobedience, **'Una hija que desobedece deja de ser hija para convertirse en enemiga'**, *(Act 3)* and all must submit to her discipline: **'Mi vigilancia lo puede todo'** *(Act 3)*.

Bernarda feels her moral code and her decisions are the right ones; the ones that correspond to the accepted social values of the time. Its rigidity does not allow any exceptions, and in Lorca's language this moral code soon becomes the type of power that will crush personal freedom, feelings and aspirations.

**Key quotation**

**Y no quiero llantos. La muerte hay que mirarla cara a cara. ¡Silencio! (*A otra hija*.) ¡A callar he dicho! (*A otra hija*.) Las lágrimas cuando estés sola. ¡Nos hundiremos en un mar de luto!**
*(Bernarda, Act 3)*

**Actividad 1**

Busca y escribe dos listas de citas de diferentes personajes. En la primera lista escribe aquellas en las que se imponga el código moral y en la segunda lista incluye aquellas contrarias a este código; ya sea porque se lamentan o porque se opongan a él. En cada caso anota quién habla.

# Repression and desire

## Love and sexual desire

This is an important theme, one which is often present in Lorca's work. Most of his protagonists suffer from an impossible or frustrated love. In *La casa de Bernarda Alba* the passion that the characters feel (mainly Adela, Martirio and María Josefa) is utterly repressed by Bernarda. These characters can't find a way out for their desire, which translates into conflict. Adela finds death, Martirio resignation and bitterness, and María Josefa is locked away.

The stallion symbolises sexual desire

Bernarda's daughters suffer from the absence of love in their lives. In addition to this, their mother is actively preventing them from marrying. Bernarda also forbids any man from coming into the house. The only one who is allowed to marry is Angustias, to Pepe el Romano, and it is his presence that causes the conflict amongst Angustias, Adela and Martirio.

**Key quotation**

ADELA. Yo soy su mujer. (*A ANGUSTIAS.*) Entérate tú y ve al corral a decírselo. El dominará toda esta casa. Ahí fuera está, respirando como si fuera un león.

ANGUSTIAS. ¡Dios mío!

BERNARDA. ¡La escopeta! ¿Dónde está la escopeta? *(Sale corriendo.)*
*(Act 3)*

In the play there are many references to love and to men: La Criada misses Bernarda's late husband, with whom she was having an affair. Poncia talks about her life with her husband, the harvesters and the prostitute that came to the town, how some men had sex with Paca la Roseta after having tied down her husband in the barn, and how la Librada's daughter met a terrible end after she killed her own illegitimate son.

Love is also the main reason why Adela commits suicide. She thinks Pepe has died and sees no other reason to be alive without him. He had become the only reason for her to live and she knows that she will never find happiness in Bernarda's house.

## Freedom through passion

Opposing this instinct of power, is the instinct of passion. However, because Bernarda refuses to communicate or discuss the issues, there is no way to reach a compromise. The family is isolated from the outside world and locked in conflict. The result of this conflict can only be the destruction of one of the opposing forces. Throughout the play Adela demonstrates an instinct for freedom:

- She carries a fan with red and green flowers instead of a black one.
- She wears a green dress.
- She is ready to run away and defy the moral code.
- She breaks one of Bernarda's sticks.
- She commits suicide out of desperation, thinking her lover has died.

**Key quotation**

*(haciéndole frente).* **¡Aquí se acabaron las voces de presidio!** ***(ADELA arrebata un bastón a su madre y lo parte en dos.)*** **Esto hago yo con la vara de la dominadora. No dé usted un paso más. ¡En mí no manda nadie más que Pepe!**

*(Adela, Act 3)*

Adela (Natalia de Azcárate) becomes increasingly desperate, leading her to rebel against the symbol of authority; Teatro Tribueñe, 2011

## Freedom through madness

María Josefa has found another way to escape Bernarda's rule: through madness. This enables her to be a voice on a more poetic and psychological level when she:

- expresses her desire for freedom
- confronts Bernarda
- denounces how Bernarda's tyranny is making everyone else suffer.

It could be deduced that neither the route of passion nor the route of madness has proved effective against Bernarda's iron rule. Only death allowed Adela's escape.

## Actividad 2

En el siguiente recuadro hay una lista de algunas de las escenas amorosas que aparecen en *La casa de Bernarda Alba*, pero no están en orden. Ponlas en orden cronológico (1-8) y añade una cita para cada una de ellas.

| Escena amorosa | Orden cronológico | Cita apropiada |
|---|---|---|
| **a)** María Josefa y el mar | | |
| **b)** La hija de la Librada | | |
| **c)** Adela declara su amor por Pepe el Romano | | |
| **d)** La Criada echa de menos a Antonio María Benavides | | |
| **e)** La mujer vestida de lentejuelas | | |
| **f)** La conversación sobre los ruidos en el corral | | |
| **g)** Martirio roba la foto de Pepe | | |
| **h)** Martirio confirma su amor por Pepe | | |

# Honour, *'el qué dirán'* and hypocrisy

Honour, *'el qué dirán'* and hypocrisy are very much connected. Honour is a question of 'keeping up appearances', making sure that family members do nothing to bring the family into disrepute, or covering up something that would be detrimental to the standing of the family were it to become known. *'El qué dirán'* is again concerned with what others might think or say, and so any circumstance which could encourage gossip has to be avoided or swept under the carpet. Hypocrisy is the pretence of having a virtuous character, or of holding moral or religious beliefs that one does not really possess; it is a means of establishing or maintaining honour and managing *'el qué dirán'*.

On reading *La casa de Bernarda Alba*, it is clear how these aspects affect the household. Bernarda's obsession with the family honour and *'el qué dirán'* is omnipresent. The first incidence we see is the obsessive cleaning she insists on because of her preoccupation with appearances.

While the funeral is in progress, Poncia and the maid are having to ensure that everything will meet Bernarda's exacting standards: **'Limpia bien todo. Si Bernarda no ve relucientes las cosas me arrancará los pocos pelos que me quedan'** *(Poncia, Act 1).*

Later, in Act 3, Bernarda insists that Angustias makes amends with Martirio when they fall out, not because she cares whether her daughters get on or not, but because of '*el qué dirán*'. She wants to keep up a façade of harmony within her house: **'Yo no me meto en los corazones, pero quiero buena fachada y armonía familiar'**.

María Josefa has to be secured with two turns of the key and a bar across the door because otherwise she might be seen by the mourners and this would cause gossip. The same point is made when Bernarda asks the maid to take María Josefa into the yard but to keep her away from the well: **'desde aquel sitio las vecinas pueden verla desde su ventana'** *(Act 1).*

Bernarda's sense of superiority over others in the village is again connected with her sense of honour: **'Hilo y aguja para las hembras. Látigo y mula para el varón. Eso tiene la gente que nace con posibles'** *(Act 1).*

For all the outward respectability of the family, we discover that Bernarda's recently-deceased husband Antonio María Benavides had indulged in an extra-marital relationship with the maid: **'Fastídiate, Antonio María Benavides, tieso con tu traje de paño y tus botas enterizas. ¡Fastídiate! ¡Ya no volverás a levantarme las enaguas detrás de la puerta de tu corral!'** *(Criada, Act 1).*

Bernarda's over-keen emphasis on honour and 'decency' causes her to hit Angustias for having looked at the men at the funeral: **'¿Es decente que una mujer de tu clase vaya con el anzuelo detrás de un hombre el día de la misa de su padre?'** *(Act 1).*

Bernarda's hypocrisy manifests itself when she wants to hear the full story of Paca la Roseta, and similarly she is very anxious to find out the gossip about la Librada's daughter.

When Adela dies, the main concern for Bernarda is honour – she insists that **'Ella, la hija menor de Bernarda Alba, ha muerto virgen. ¿Me habéis oído?'** *(Act 3).*

**Actividad 3**

Considera el tema del honor y de *el qué dirán*. Escribe unas 250 palabras en español en las que expliques su significado y cuándo ocurre en el drama.

## Tradition – the role of women

In *La casa de Bernarda Alba*, we see that Lorca has incorporated a number of features typical for a woman in the 1930s in Andalusia, elsewhere in Spain and in other parts of the world. For example, when it came to marriage it was the oldest daughter who had priority. This accounts for why Pepe would only be acceptable to Bernarda as a husband for her oldest daughter Angustias and not for Adela, in spite of the fact that this is where there is a strong attraction.

Bernarda expects the girls to spend the eight years of mourning preparing their trousseaus – clothes and household linens – which they would take to their home on marriage. It was the responsibility of the mother to ensure that there was a trousseau and this would also include furniture as we see in the play. Furniture has already been acquired for Angustias' forthcoming marriage: **'Mientras, podéis empezar a bordaros el ajuar. En el arca tengo veinte piezas de hilo con el que podréis cortar sabanas y embozos'** *(Act 1).* And when she tells Prudencia about the furniture she has purchased for Angustias:

**'PRUDENCIA. Los muebles me han dicho que son preciosos.**

**BERNARDA. Dieciséis mil reales he gastado.**

**PONCIA.** ***(interviniendo)*** **Lo mejor es el armario de luna'** *(Act 3).*

In society at this time there was no equality of the sexes. Men dominated and there was a clear delineation of duties and jobs. As Bernarda says, **'Hilo y aguja para las hembras. Látigo y mula para el varón'** *(Act 1).*

The class system was also very clearly defined and although Bernarda's behaviour is excessive, there was a greater gap between different classes than there are today, and greater concern about not marrying 'beneath your class'. It is important to understand that this is not a distinction based purely on wealth (Bernarda's family are wealthier than others in the village as they own land) but also on pretentions of respect and reputation. Bernarda feels her family are more reputable than others, and this is what she is trying desperately to preserve when she imposes the strict moral code.

The question of mourning and the traditions around it have changed considerably. The tradition for a long period of mourning was widespread, though nowhere near as draconian as the eight years imposed on her daughters by Bernarda. The norm in Andalusia at that time was in the region of one year for a widower and two years for a widow, although it would not have been imposed on the children to the same extent. It is worth noting that in rural Spain in particular, the tradition for a widow to continue indefinitely wearing black was widespread up to the last decades of the twentieth century.

One final tradition that was of paramount importance, but is no longer the case in Western Europe, was the preservation of a woman's virginity until marriage. Likewise, to have a child out of wedlock was a disgrace. Nowadays, over 40% of babies in Spain are born to unmarried couples.

### Actividad 4

Considera cómo ha cambiado el papel de la mujer en España desde los años 30 del siglo veinte. Puedes considerar, por ejemplo:

- sus labores en el hogar
- su incorporación al mundo laboral
- sus derechos
- su libertad sexual.

Si es posible, comparte tus ideas con un(a) compañero/a.

## Actividad 5

Lee el artículo 'Ser mujer en *La casa de Bernarda Alba*'.
Responde a las preguntas en español de forma breve y concisa. No es necesario hacer frases completas en todas las respuestas.

### Ser mujer en *La casa de Bernarda Alba*

De entre los temas que se tratan en esta obra de teatro me gustaría centrarme en el de las mujeres, en cómo vivían y eran tratadas y qué es lo que nos revela esta obra de Lorca.

Para empezar, tenemos a Bernarda, la señora de la casa, que se parece a una reina de la edad media, con poder casi absoluto sobre sus súbditos. Decide cuánto tiempo durará el luto, es decir, por cuánto tiempo tienen que estar encerradas en la casa. También es la que decide con quién se casarán sus hijas y con quién no y ¡Ay de quién la contradiga!

Otro elemento que no puedo dejar de ignorar es la falta de trabajo y de educación. Las cinco hijas de Bernarda solo cosen, durante todo el día esa es su única actividad y distracción. No es de extrañar que Magdalena prefiera el destino de los varones, el de trabajar duro. Claro que podría haber ayudado a Poncia o a la Criada, porque ellas no descansan ni de día ni de noche, pero ni eso les estaba permitido por ser ellas de clase social más alta.

Mujeres tiranas, otras prisioneras, otras siempre atareadas y todas sin poder decidir su destino. Un destino dramático ser mujer en *La casa de Bernarda Alba*.

1. ¿En qué se centra este artículo?
2. ¿Con quién compara a Bernarda Alba?
3. Bernarda tiene mucho poder. Menciona dos ejemplos de lo que puede decidir en su casa.
4. ¿Qué dos problemas graves menciona el artículo?
5. ¿Por qué prefiere Magdalena el destino de los hombres?
6. ¿Por qué no les dejaban ayudar a las criadas?
7. ¿Por qué dice el artículo que era dramático nacer mujer en la casa de Bernarda? Menciona dos razones.

# The role of men

There are no visible male characters in the drama although those referred to actually play pivotal roles, especially Pepe el Romano. He is the catalyst of all the events of the play which cause conflict and hatred amongst the sisters:

- his proposal to Angustias – the richest of the daughters
- his betrayal of Angustias with Adela
- the feelings Martirio has for him.

Because of the actions of men, Paca la Roseta is marginalised and the daughter of la Librada is treated shockingly. Those male characters, although not actually appearing in the play, illustrate the extreme views of the society of the day and underline the inequality of rights faced by women and the supremacy of men. For example, the men who took Paca to the olive grove and the father of the illegitimate child were not the subject of vilification. They were not condemned for their interest in sex and for having extramarital relations because that was considered acceptable, as was the young reaper arranging to have the services of a prostitute.

## Actividad 6

Explica brevemente quiénes son estos hombres mencionados en la obra.

**a)** Antonio María Benavides

**b)** Pepe el Romano

**c)** Enrique Humanes

**d)** Evaristo el Colorín

**e)** Los segadores

**f)** Don Arturo

## Actividad 7

Lee atentamente el artículo 'El viaje a *La casa de Bernarda Alba*'.

**1.** Busca en los párrafos 2 y 3 palabras o frases que signifiquen lo mismo que:

**a)** debo

**b)** inaguantable

**c)** la ausencia

**d)** permitió

**e)** ir a rezar

**f)** contó

**g)** observaba con atención

**h)** el varón con mejor tipo

**i)** parar

**j)** me hizo sentir muy triste

2. Traduce el último párrafo del artículo de abajo.

**El viaje a *La casa de Bernarda Alba***

Hora de llegada: doce del mediodía: lugar un pueblo de Andalucía, en la provincia de Granada. Misión: entrevistarme con Bernarda Alba y con su antítesis Adela.

Tengo que decir que la primera impresión fue la de un calor abrasador, y la falta de aire acondicionado lo hacía casi insoportable. Me vestí como una mujer de mediana edad de la época, es decir de color negro, pero al llegar a la famosa casa de Bernarda, su criada no me dejó entrar, me dijo que su dueña era una mujer mandona y autoritaria que no permitiría que nadie saliera de la casa en ocho años, excepto para ir a misa los domingos.

Como no me rindo tan fácilmente, el domingo fui a la iglesia y tuve la suerte de poder sentarme al lado de Adela. Ella me dijo que llevaba un abanico verde y rojo en su bolso pero que no se atrevía a usarlo porque su madre siempre las vigilaba a ella y a sus hermanas. Le pregunté por Pepe el Romano y me dijo que era el hombre más guapo del pueblo, que no podía dejar de pensar en él y que haría todo lo que fuera necesario para estar con él. Me dio mucha lástima porque no me está permitido dar consejos que puedan cambiar la historia literaria. ¿Qué le habrías dicho tú a Adela?

## Society in the play

In *La casa de Bernarda Alba* we see a society where there is a clearly-defined social structure. Women are to be married off with a **dowry** and if you happen to have a substantial inheritance that would make your dowry all the more attractive to a prospective suitor, as happens between Angustias and Pepe. Servants know their place and migrant workers come and go with the seasons – think of the association between the reapers and summer. Notions of the value of a person are tied to wealth, gender and perceived status/class. In the play we can see what happens when a person strays from this strict societal structure.

**dowry** *la dote* the money and goods that a wife brings to her husband at marriage

## Social injustice and class

Bernarda represents the traditional values of Spain; Teatro Tribueñe, 2011

Although the play does not directly comment on the socio-economic problems of Spain in 1936, it does reflect them and we can read in its lines a strong social protest. Lorca can be seen to be criticising the conservative class for allowing its injustices.

Bernarda represents the conservative class that was used to giving commands and abusing its power, lacking empathy and noble values, and that despised the lower social classes. In many ways, the play is a metaphor for the social situation of Spain at that time. Bernarda wants to impose her old-fashioned ideas on her household and the thick walls of the house represent the prison-like environment in which they live.

**Key quotation**

**En ocho años que dure el luto no ha de entrar en esta casa el viento de la calle. Haceros cuenta que hemos tapiado con ladrillos puertas y ventanas. Así pasó en casa de mi padre y en casa de mi abuelo.**
*(Bernarda, Act 1)*

When Bernarda worries about the family honour, she is showing an elitist attitude that is especially aimed at the marriage of her daughters and to how she treats her servants. She forbade the marriage between Martirio and Enrique Humanes because he belonged to a lower social class: '**¿Es que quieres que se las entregue a cualquier gañán?**' *(Act 1).* Bernarda perceives her world as a highly-structured society: marriage is not to be chosen, it is something that is arranged.

**Actividad 8**

El honor es de gran importancia para Bernarda Alba y hace todo lo posible para preservarlo. Encuentra cinco ejemplos en la obra que muestren la obsesión de Bernarda con el honor y la tradición.

## Social hierarchy

The play describes a social **hierarchy** that the characters accept and do not try to change. Remember that Adela only wants to change Bernarda's authority for Pepe's, and María Josefa wants to remarry; in terms of social hierarchy, simply maintaining the **status quo**. All human relations are hierarchised and characterised by the cruelty of their immediate superiors as well as by their resignation to this rule.

Poncia describes her position as: **'Pero soy yo buena perra'** *(Act 1)* – resignation that is tainted with hatred. All the characters tend to humiliate those in a lower class to themselves, as even the servant humiliates the beggar: **'Por la puerta se va a la calle. Las sobras de hoy son para mí'** *(Act 1).*

In the highest position of the hierarchy we have Bernarda, followed by Angustias, who is the oldest daughter and the wealthiest. After them we have the rest of the daughters, María Josefa, Poncia, the servant and finally the beggar, who represents human injustice and abject poverty. Within the house, wealth is an element of the class distinction. This contrast between poverty and wealth can be seen in the first scene, in the dialogue between Poncia and the servant.

**Key quotation**

**PONCIA. Nosotras tenemos nuestras manos y un hoyo en la tierra de la verdad.**

**CRIADA. Esa es la única tierra que nos dejan a los que no tenemos nada.**
*(Act 1)*

The difference in wealth affects Bernarda's daughters as only Angustias is going to marry and this is because of her substantial inheritance. Pepe el Romano chooses Angustias even when he desires Adela.

**hierarchy** *la jerarquía* any system of persons or things ranked one above another

**status quo** *statu quo* the existing state of affairs

## The effect of social conflict

The conflict of traditional and new social ideas within the play is demonstrated in the profound effects it has on each of the daughters. For example, Martirio appears twisted and poisoned by the disappointment in her life, caused by her mother's social objections to her love interest. Adela feels trapped and abandoned within her social confines and without even the love of her sisters for comfort.

**Key quotation**

**MARTIRIO. Tengo el corazón lleno de una fuerza tan mala, que, sin quererlo yo, a mí misma me ahoga.**

**ADELA. Nos enseñan a querer a las hermanas. Dios me ha debido dejar sola, en medio de la oscuridad, porque te veo como si no te hubiera visto nunca.**
*(Act 3)*

However, if we read carefully what Adela says to Martirio in Act 3, it seems that she is ready to live under someone else's authority: Pepe's.

**Key quotation**

**Ya no aguanto el horror de estos techos después de haber probado el sabor de su boca. Seré lo que él quiera que sea [...], y me pondré delante de todos la corona de espinas que tienen las que son queridas de algún hombre casado.**

*(Adela, Act 3)*

This would suggest then that she is not Lorca's symbol of change; that she does in fact ultimately comply with the tradition that a woman should live under the **subjugation** of her parents or a man.

**Actividad 9**

Considera estas dos afirmaciones. ¿Hasta qué punto estás de acuerdo con cada una de ellas?

**a)** Adela no es un personaje que quiere la libertad – cambiaría la autoridad de su madre por la de Pepe.

**b)** Adela lucha por tener la libertad de elegir. Se le negó el derecho de amar al hombre que quería y el derecho de dejar la casa de su madre.

**subjugation** *el sometimiento* the act of bringing someone under complete control

The play also shows the social conflict between two generations. On the one side, we have the conservative generation, very strict and blinded by the traditional concept of honour, represented by Bernarda. On the other, we have her daughters who represent a new generation who wants to live in a different way.

## Hatred and jealousy

Most of the relationships in the play are influenced by hatred and jealousy. The women live imprisoned in an unfriendly and closed environment. The desire for freedom and love, as well as the frustration at not having them, make the characters frequently bitter and confrontational. The quarrelsome and progressively cruel exchanges between Martirio and Adela are an example of this. Poncia and the servant hate Bernarda, and Poncia describes her as *mandona, dominanta* and *tirana.*

Bernarda is also hated by her daughters, her own mother (who calls her *Bernarda cara de leoparda)* and even the family of her late husband, who do not attend the funeral because they can't stand her. There are many references to hatred in the stage directions, such as *con odio* and *con sarcasmo.*

**Key quotation**

**¡No me abraces! No quieras ablandar mis ojos. Mi sangre ya no es la tuya, y aunque quisiera verte como hermana no te miro ya más que como mujer. (*La rechaza*.)**
*(Martirio, Act 3)*

**Actividad 10**

Encuentra más ejemplos de cómo Lorca expresa el odio en la obra.

Jealousy is also present in the play. This is predominantly expressed between Bernarda's daughters, especially Adela and Martirio. They envy Angustias' wealth but also the fact that she will soon marry and be able to escape Bernarda's domination. Curiously, they do not feel jealous because she will marry the man that they love, because they both know that Pepe does not love her and that he only wants her money: **'No te importa que abrace a la que no quiere. A mí tampoco'** *(Adela, Act 3)*.

It is Martirio who symbolises jealousy and its destructive nature. Firstly, it makes her refuse her sisterhood with Adela, but by the end of Act 3 it has driven her to lie to Adela and say that Pepe has died, **'Se acabó Pepe el Romano'** *(Act 3)*, which in turn pushes Adela to kill herself.

Interestingly there is no jealousy between the different classes because they accept their place with resignation. There is even gratitude, for example, when we find out that Poncia's son works as a farmer on Bernarda's land.

## Writing about themes

In order to succeed in the exam you need to be familiar with the themes and be able to differentiate between the major and the minor ones. You could well be expected to discuss one or two specific themes but equally you could be asked a question along the lines of '*En tu opinión ¿cuál es el tema más importante del drama?*' which requires a thorough knowledge and an ability to substantiate your argument.

Even if the question is not specifically about themes, you still need to understand them. For example, if you were writing about one of the major characters you would need to include their relevance to the themes of the play in your answer. For example, you could hardly discuss Bernarda without reference to honour, '*el qué dirán*', hypocrisy, relationships and the role of women. If you were talking about Adela then you would need to refer to the themes of freedom, rebellion, love and passion.

## Actividad 11

1. Pon las siguientes afirmaciones sobre la obra de teatro según tu grado de preferencia, comenzando con la que estés más de acuerdo y terminando con la que menos.

   **a)** Es una crítica social hecha desde el punto de vista de una persona perteneciente a una clase media liberal, contra la moral agobiante que imperaba en la sociedad rural.

   **b)** Se desarrolla en un mundo que Lorca conoce y ama, lleno de violencia y pasión – la realidad de Andalucía.

   **c)** Lorca usa el mito de Andalucía – calor, pasión, contrastes, violencia – para darle a su obra un sabor regional.

   **d)** Lorca ubica su obra en la España rural para que su público reconozca y empatice con un mundo familiar.

   **e)** La obra no trata sobre personajes individuales sino sobre diferentes aspectos psicológicos que surgen del conflicto entre el deseo y la represión.

   **f)** La obra se centra en los conflictos generacionales en un momento de cambio social.

   **g)** La obra trata del conflicto entre la pasión y las reglas de la sociedad.

   **h)** El lenguaje de la obra es realista y asequible.

   **i)** Este drama es una obra de arte maestra que usa el lenguaje y los efectos visuales magistralmente.

   **j)** La obra es una mezcla decepcionante de realidad y poesía, que da la impresión de no estar bien desarrollada ni acabada.

   **k)** Existe una evolución gradual en la obra en la que se comienza describiendo el mundo real y que desemboca siendo una obra poética y simbólica.

2. A continuación escribe un párrafo sobre los tres últimos puntos, es decir, los que *menos* te hayan gustado. Añade citas para explicar por qué no estás de acuerdo con esas ideas.

3. Como habrás imaginado, ahora es el momento de hacer exactamente lo opuesto. Escribe un párrafo sobre tus tres puntos favoritos.

## Vocabulary

**los celos/la envidia** jealousy

**el conflicto** conflict

**el enfrentamiento** confrontation

**la hipocresía** hypocrisy

**la locura** madness

**el odio** hatred

**la pasión** passion

**la protesta social** social protest

**la reputación** reputation

**el suicidio** suicide

**la superioridad** superiority

**la tradición** tradition

## Useful phrases

**Se crea una impresión de...** An impression of ... is created

**Este tema está estrechamente conectado con...** This theme is closely connected to...

**No es posible hablar del tema de las mujeres sin mencionar...** It is not possible to discuss the theme of women without mentioning...

**Este tema se ilustra a través de...** This theme is illustrated by...

**Para comprender cómo se representa la libertad en la obra, es necesario...** To understand the representation of freedom in the play, it is necessary to...

**Voy a centrarme en el tema de...** I will focus on the theme of...

**Un acontecimiento que resalta este tema es...** An episode which highlights this theme is...

**Lorca enfatiza este tema [+ gerund]...** Lorca emphasises this theme by...

**Además de este punto, voy a examinar el tema de...** As well as this point, I am going to examine the theme of...

## Before you start

The first rule is, understandably, to know your text thoroughly. While studying the text and then in your revision, take note of the following points:

- You need to know the plot and the correct sequence of events. This is where a short summary will be helpful, but remember that this is no substitute for having an in-depth knowledge of the play. No summary will contain all the action.
- Do not rely only on an English translation. Although this can of course be useful, it is not what you are studying: you are studying the original work, the language, vocabulary and nuances of that version and not the translation.
- Know the characters – for example:
    - their personalities
    - their relationships with each other
    - the motives for their behaviour.
- Make sure that you have an understanding of the context in which the work is set, and how it relates to the play itself.
- Revise what you have learned about the structure of the play and its language.
- Learn a selection of quotations.

With all that knowledge under your belt you should be well-equipped to tackle any question.

When you read the exam paper, take note of practicalities. What is the time allocation? What is the mark allocation? None of these should come as a surprise to you and you should have had sufficient essay-writing practice to know exactly how many words you need to write to fulfil the requirements. Do not write more than 10% more or fewer words than the stated number.

If you have two essays to write, be very careful to allow sufficient time for the second one.

## Understanding the question

Read the options very carefully. Consider *exactly* what they are asking for. Look at the key words the question contains because you must do what you are asked to do and not what you would *like* to do! For example:

| | |
|---|---|
| *Analiza* | Analyse |
| *Cómo* | How |
| *Describe* | Describe |
| *Compara* | Compare |
| *Examina* | Examine |
| *Explica* | Explain |
| *Evalúa* | Evaluate |
| *Explora* | Explore |
| *Hasta qué punto* | To what extent |
| *En tu opinión* | In your opinion |
| *Justifica* | Justify |

If the question were to say, for example, '*Analiza el carácter de Bernarda*' then this will need to be tackled in greater depth than '*Describe el carácter de Bernarda*'. You would still be expected to explore the topic in detail if asked to describe, including presenting evidence from the text and using contextual knowledge to demonstrate an understanding of the text, but a question which requires *analysis* means you must do more than give information; you must interpret it from your own point of view.

If you are asked to *justify* your views, this means saying what you think and defending those views. As a rule, this is something you should always do in an exam answer, even if the question does not include the word '*justifica*'.

'*En tu opinión*', like '*justifica*', needs an explanation of why you think as you do, with clear supporting evidence.

If the question demands a comparison, make sure that you give equal weight to both sides before reaching a conclusion.

'*Hasta qué punto*' will require a balance between two or more ways of looking at an issue but these need not necessarily be equal – for example, if the question were: '*¿Hasta qué punto fue Bernarda responsable del suicidio de Adela?*' you would need to bring in other factors that contributed to her suicide which might involve Bernarda, Martirio, Pepe, and Adela herself, before concluding which, if any, single factor bears the responsibility.

All questions will require you to construct a strong argument to support your views. Always analyse and evaluate what you are writing. You may be familiar with the format of Point-Evidence-Explanation (PEE) which is a good place to start, but at AS and A Level you will be expected to write in a more sophisticated way to help you achieve this. When you make a point, it should be accurate and detailed, using opinion or other views. Support it with relevant and precise quotations from or references to the play. Finally, go on to explain but also analyse its relevance to the argument you are making, commenting on issue, theme or context, for example.

# Planning your answer

Having decided which of the options you are going to take, spend a little time thinking and planning what you are going to say. Do not dive straight in and start writing immediately even if other people around you seem to be writing away furiously! Effort made at this point on careful planning will lead to more efficient use of time and help you achieve better marks.

Here is one way you might approach the planning:

1. Reread the question to make sure that you know exactly what is being asked of you.
2. Quickly jot down bullet points of things you need to include. It is a good idea to write your notes in Spanish; that way you can be sure you know all the necessary vocabulary before you begin writing your essay.
3. Although there is no hard and fast rule about the number of points you are going to make, remember that you have a limit of around 300 words. To make a point adequately and justify it will take 40–50 words as a rough estimate. With the introduction and conclusion taken into account you can only logically expect to make four or five substantial points, so what you say has to be good!
4. If the question requires two points to be addressed, make two lists.
5. Indicate where you can insert quotations and make sure that you can justify everything you say with an explanation or a quotation.
6. Number your points in what you consider to be the best order for covering them. If you have too many points, eliminate the weakest or combine several together if you can.
7. Now that you are clear what you are going to say, it is time to write your essay. First, consider your **introduction**, which should be brief but it must show the reader (the examiner) that your answer is going to be relevant.

   Secondly, write the **body of your essay** (see advice for this below).

   Finally, having covered all your points, your **conclusion** should briefly sum them up and give a judgement or decision on the subject. You should not introduce anything new in the conclusion.

## Spider diagrams

There are many ways to plan your essay: bullet-pointed lists, concept maps, flow charts or spider diagrams. Whatever style you use, do take the trouble to also number points in the order in which you intend to cover them. This will give your finished essay a more cohesive structure and will also mean that you don't inadvertently miss anything out.

Here is the start of a spider-diagram plan for the following exam-style question:

> Considera los métodos que Lorca utiliza en la trama de *La casa de Bernarda Alba* para reflejar la represión en España.

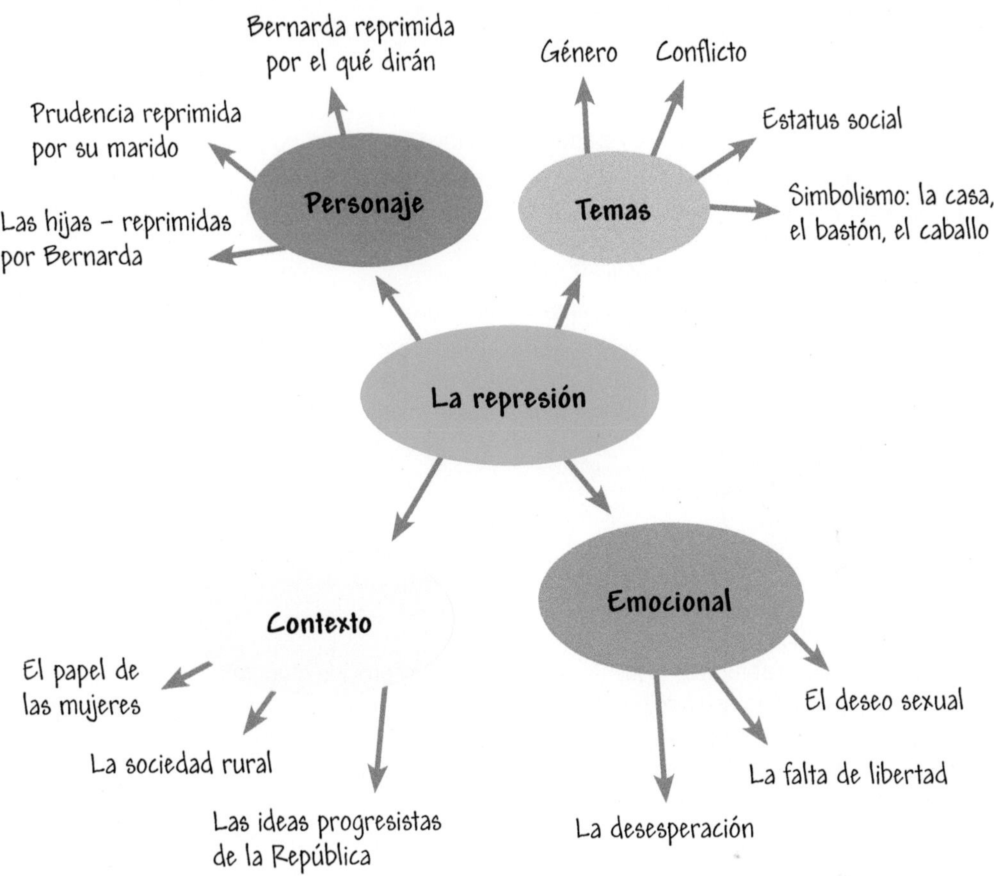


## Tips for assessment

Upgrade

It doesn't matter which planning method you use, the important thing is to make sure you *do* create a plan before you write. Try out different methods when you are revising and find out which works best for you. You might find different approaches work better for different types of question.

# Writing your answer

Look at the clock and work out when your essay should be finished. Allow as much time as possible (5–10 minutes) for careful checking at the end.

- Write your introductory paragraph.
- Following the order in your plan, work through your points. Generally speaking, each point will occupy one paragraph.
- Each point should be coherently explained and justified with evidence from the text. When you can, give a quotation but make sure it is relevant and not too long, otherwise it will eat into your word allowance. If you aren't using a quotation, make sure you describe accurately what is said in the text to back up your point.
- As you come to the end of each paragraph, refer back to the title of the essay. This will ensure that what you are writing is relevant. Be careful when looking at contrasting arguments not to appear to constantly contradict yourself. Explain when you are exploring a point of view.
- Use a wide range of vocabulary and sentence structures.
- Use your checking time productively and critically to proofread your work. Establish your own check-list which might include the following, but should be based on the areas where you yourself tend to make mistakes:
  - verb tenses and endings
  - adjectival agreements
  - spellings and genders
  - use of the subjunctive.

## Using quotations

Quotations are a very useful way of justifying a point as they provide proof from the text. Their appropriate use also demonstrates that you have a good working knowledge of the text, and this will be recognised by the examiner. However, indiscriminate use of quotations just to prove that you learned them is of no value and is actually counter-productive.

As you study the play, note down textual references to illustrate all the themes, all the characters, and so on. Note the page numbers where you found them so that you can easily refer back to them in your revision. Do not try to learn long quotations – it is difficult to do and in any case they will take up space you might well need. More and shorter is the key: a well-chosen word or phrase can be far more effective than a long, rambling quotation.

### Tips for assessment

Make a conscious effort to learn relevant and succinct quotations. Do this little by little to make it a more achievable goal.

There are many pertinent quotations in this literary companion to help you begin building a strong reference list, but do not restrict yourself to these – there are plenty more which you can find for yourself.

### Tips for assessment

In order to achieve high marks for your essay you need to do the following:

- Use excellent Spanish, which will include a wide range of vocabulary and accurately-applied grammatical structures.
- Show a thorough knowledge and understanding of the text, which will involve not simply knowing what happens but being able to see the bigger picture, including analysis of symbolism, structure and language.
- Write a totally relevant answer to the question.
- Provide substantiating evidence for your points, i.e. detailed reference to the text and/or pertinent quotations.
- Remember that your own views and opinions are valid even if different from the mainstream, *provided that you can justify them.*

**Useful phrases**

**To introduce your argument:**
Para empezar…; En primer lugar…; Voy a hablar sobre…; Voy a analizar…; Se puede considerar…; Uno de los … más importantes es…

**To link a series of points together:**
y; así como; además; también; o; no solo … sino que; tanto uno … como otro

**To introduce a new subject:**
Hay que considerar también…; No hay que olvidar a/que…; Debemos recordar que…; No se debe pasar por alto que…

**To give an example:**
por ejemplo…; esto se puede ver en…; la obra nos muestra como…; otro ejemplo es cuando…

**To give an explanation:**
esto significa que…; esto quiere decir que…; esto sugiere que…; esto nos muestra que…; esto me hace pensar que…

**To explain why:**
porque; ya que; puesto que; debido a; como consecuencia; por tanto; así que

**To give an opinion:**
creo que…; pienso que…; a mi modo de ver…; a mi juicio…; desde mi punto de vista…; me parece que…; diría que…

**To argue an opposite view:**
Por otra parte…; Por el contrario…; Desde otro punto de vista…

**To concede a point:**
Hay que admitir…; Hay que tener en cuenta que…

**To sum up:**
En resumen…; En resumidas cuentas…; Para resumir…

**To conclude:**
En conclusión; Para concluir; Para terminar

# Sample questions

## AS

1

Describe y compara los papeles de dos de los personajes de la obra.

Puedes mencionar a:

- Bernarda
- María Josefa
- Poncia
- Pepe el Romano.

**2**

Escoge un tema de la obra y explica por qué es importante. A continuación describe cómo lo representa Lorca.

Puedes mencionar:

- el honor
- el amor
- la tradición
- la rebeldía.

**3**

Examina las distintas personalidades de dos o tres de las cinco hijas de Bernarda Alba. ¿Merecen nuestra simpatía?

Puedes mencionar a:

- Angustias
- Martirio
- Magdalena
- Adela
- Amelia.

## A Level

**1**

Analiza el papel de María Josefa en ***La casa de Bernarda Alba***. ¿Qué quiere Lorca que represente y cómo cumple su intención?

**2**

Considera los personajes invisibles de la obra. En tu opinión, ¿qué importancia tienen?

**3**

Analiza los temas del honor y de la reputación en ***La casa de Bernarda Alba***. ¿Hasta qué punto contribuyen al suicidio de Adela?

**4**

Discute el uso de tres símbolos en la obra. ¿Cuál te parece que ha contribuido más a la obra? Justifica tu respuesta.

**5**

Hay temas en ***La casa de Bernarda Alba*** que tienen relevancia hoy en día. ¿Hasta qué punto estás de acuerdo con esta afirmación?

# Sample answers

## Sample answer 1: AS

Describe la personalidad de Bernarda y examina su relación con sus hijas. Puedes mencionar a:

- Amelia
- Angustias
- Adela
- Martirio.

*Bernarda es una madre autoritaria que no escucha a sus hijas y que solo se preocupa por su reputación.*

Good introductory sentence.

*Al principio de la obra Poncia la llama "dominanta y mandona" porque todo el mundo que vive en su casa debe obedecerle, por ejemplo, la casa debe estar limpia, sin una mota de polvo. Su primera y última palabra es la misma orden, "¡Silencio!". Bernarda es una tirana no solo con sus sirvientas, sino también con sus hijas. Decide que deben pasar ocho años de luto por la muerte de su marido Antonio María Benavides y también es cruel ya que en el primer acto golpea e insulta a su hija mayor Angustias por llevar maquillaje y a Martirio en el segundo. "¡Mala puñalada te den, mosca muerta!" "¡Sembradura de vidrios!"*

This sentence clearly describes her dominance and obsession with cleanliness.

Accurate language and good attention to detail.

Appropriate quotation that exemplifies her cruelty and despotic attitude towards her daughters.

*Bernarda está obsesionada por 'el qué dirán' y por eso encierra a su propia madre, María Josefa, para que sus vecinos no descubran que padece demencia. Sabe que sus hijas no son felices, pero no le importa, siempre y cuando se comporten: "Yo no me meto en los corazones, pero quiero buena fachada y armonía familiar".*

Appropriate use of the subjunctive mood.

*Tiene una relación muy complicada con su hija menor, Adela, que es su antítesis, ya que ella quiere ser libre, salir de casa y aborrece la idea de ir vestida de luto. Bernarda está obsesionada con la honra, pero a Adela lo único que le importa es el amor y estar con Pepe el Romano ya que desea ser su amante, es decir, rechaza la decencia y la moralidad de la época. Bernarda representa la represión con su bastón – "golpea con su bastón" – sin embargo*

Starts addressing the second half of the question, focusing on one of the daughters.

This section cleverly combines information for both halves of the question.

This sentence explains well how Bernarda's concern with *'el qué dirán'* shapes her relationship with Adela.

A concise and pertinent conclusion where no new ideas have been introduced.

*Adela lo rompe y así desafía su autoridad. Al final de la obra, Bernarda solo se preocupa de que todos piensen que su hija ha muerto virgen: "Ella, la hija menor de Bernarda Alba, ha muerto virgen".*

*En conclusión, Bernarda es un personaje que encarna el poder ciego, mantiene una relación de opresión con sus hijas y es capaz de todo para proteger su decencia sin tener en cuenta los sentimientos de nadie.*

This is a good essay. The candidate has addressed both parts of the question as fully as possible within the recommended number of words and shows a thorough knowledge of the text. The use of language and grammar is accurate.

## Sample answer 2: AS

Describe varios de los símbolos que utiliza Lorca. En tu opinión ¿cuáles te han impresionado más? Puedes mencionar:

- el caballo
- los colores
- el bastón
- el agua.

Good introductory sentence.

Poor attempt at addressing the second half of the question.

This is potentially good but it is a shame that the candidate did not develop this answer.

This is an ambiguous sentence.

A good symbol, well justified, with an appropriate quotation.

*Federico García Lorca usa muchos símbolos en su obra que son muy interesantes y que hacen que sea muy buena.*

*Me gustó mucho el símbolo del agua porque representa muchas cosas diferentes en la historia. Por ejemplo, el pozo representa la falta de libertad y sin embargo el mar representa la libertad. Me gustan mucho porque Adela dice que 'tiene sed' lo que significa que tiene deseo sexual.*

*Otro símbolo muy bonito es el caballo garañón, es blanco y quiere ser libre. Quiere estar con las yeguas así que también representa la libertad y el deseo sexual: "El caballo garañón … da coces contra el muro". Me encanta porque Bernarda tiene muchos caballos pero no tiene la felicidad.*

Irrelevant; with a restricted word count it is vital to make every point count.

*El escritor usa elementos de la naturaleza como símbolos, por ejemplo las perlas del anillo de Agustina son lágrimas, Prudencia dice, "En mi tiempo las perlas significaban lágrimas", la noche es el misterio y el drama, el sol es el hombre, por ejemplo los segadores trabajan cuando hace mucho sol.*

The ideas of this paragraph are good, with references to several natural symbols, however the punctuation causes some difficulty.

*La obra sucede en verano, en pleno agosto, es importante porque el calor representa la opresión. Las hijas no pueden salir de casa porque hay un luto y no tenían aire acondicionado en esa época. No me gustaría vivir en una casa tan opresiva en España.*

Good ideas but needs better accuracy.

This is irrelevant.

*La casa también es un símbolo que representa una prisión porque las hijas no pueden salir. Tiene 'muros gruesos' y es monocromática, es decir, solo hay color blanco. Todo está muy limpio porque Bernarda tiene dos sirvientas. Hace un contraste con el negro que representa la muerte y la tristeza porque es el color del luto.*

A good point has been made and justified, but the comment on the servants is irrelevant.

*En conclusión el autor usa muchos símbolos para mantener la tensión y para hacer su historia más interesante y divertida.*

Poor conclusion which does not refer back to the title.

This is a poor essay. It doesn't fully address the question as it doesn't say which symbol impressed the candidate the most. Also, there are several irrelevant comments. Vocabulary is limited and repetitive at times. The grammar is predominantly accurate but the choice of language is of GCSE level. However, there are some attempts at more advanced structures.

## Sample answer 3: A Level

Lorca nos advierte en su lista de personajes que *La casa de Bernarda Alba* es 'un documental fotográfico'. ¿Hasta qué punto logró su objetivo?

*Lorca describe su obra como un documental fotográfico. Para lograrlo retrata la vida diaria de las habitantes de la casa, la lentitud de la acción y usa una cromática similar a las de las fotografías de la época. Ahora voy a analizar si tuvo éxito en su intento.*

Precise and pertinent introduction which comes straight to the point of the question; language is accurate.

*Lorca capta la vida diaria dentro de la casa, como si se tratara de una serie de fotografías, por ejemplo, la vida rutinaria de estas mujeres, como cuando la Criada y Poncia trabajan en la casa o cuando las hijas de Bernarda cosen el ajuar de*

Candidate answers with a relevant point dealing with the daily routine which can be captured photographically.

Good development of the techniques used by Lorca to convey the slow passing of time – as photographs are static.

*Angustias. Otro elemento que nos conduce a pensar que se trata de fotografías es la lentitud de la acción, ya que estas son estáticas. Es decir, es como si el tiempo pasara más lentamente dentro de la casa, por ejemplo cuando Martirio dice "este verano interminable", se refiere a que los días parecen infinitos.*

A comprehensive explanation of the photographic resemblance of this play.

An insightful remark which shows a perceptive approach to the text.

*La característica cromática de la casa es el blanco y el negro, tal y como las fotos de la época. Las acotaciones nos describen una casa con muros blancos y con habitaciones blancas ('habitación blanquísima') que contrastan con el negro de la ropa de las mujeres que deben vestirse de luto durante ocho años. Solo hay pequeñas islas de color, como el abanico de Adela y su vestido verde. Retocar las fotos con algo de color era habitual. Otro elemento a tener en cuenta es cuando Martirio roba la foto de Pepe parece como si fuera una foto dentro de otra foto, es muy ingenioso.*

Good argument against his level of success, adding depth to the essay.

Relevant quotation to justify a valid point.

*Pero no todo parece un documental fotográfico, por ejemplo, los personajes invisibles que tanta influencia tienen en la obra, como Pepe el Romano, no pueden aparecer en una fotografía porque no se ven. Además, una fotografía no puede transmitir los temas esenciales de la obra como el deseo de Adela "por encima de mi madre saltaría para apagarme este fuego que tengo levantado por piernas y boca", la envidia de Martirio ni la obsesión de Bernarda por el qué dirán, que son temas fundamentales.*

A concise conclusion which sums up the answer to the question.

*En conclusión, Lorca solo consigue que su obra parezca un documental fotográfico en la estética y en la vida cotidiana de esas mujeres, pero la obra no es un documental en su totalidad porque es imposible que la técnica fotográfica capture los temas de la obra ni a algunos de sus personajes.*

This is a very good essay showing skilful manipulation of language and deep knowledge of the text. It includes a wide range of relevant examples and it has pertinent quotations to exemplify points made. The question has been addressed and the essay has a good structure. For the most part, syntax is quite sophisticated and the vocabulary used is appropriate and varied.

## Sample answer 4: A Level

¿Qué fuerzas llevaron al suicidio de Adela? ¿Fue inevitable su muerte?

*Existen varias razones que llevaron a Adela al suicidio. La más obvia es la supuesta muerte de Pepe el Romano pero también influyen otras circunstancias como la autoridad represiva de Bernarda, la envidia de sus hermanas y el posible embarazo de Adela.*

*Cuando Martirio le dice a Adela que Bernarda ha matado a Pepe, Adela se desespera porque piensa que nunca podrá estar con el hombre que ama y se suicida. Para empezar Adela está enamorada de él, como se puede ver cuando dice que tiene sed, lo que alude a su deseo sexual insatisfecho.*

*Adela es la antítesis de Bernarda. Luchan porque Bernarda impone un luto de ocho años, por lo que Adela no puede buscar un hombre, ni salir de casa y su única posibilidad de escapar y de encontrar el amor desaparece con la muerte de Pepe: "¡No quiero perder mi blancura en estas habitaciones!"*

*Otra razón es que Adela no se lleva bien con sus hermanas, por ejemplo, Martirio que también está enamorada de Pepe el Romano. Es ella quien alerta a su madre cuando Adela quiere escapar con él y también le dice a Adela que Pepe ha muerto. Es una mentira cruel motivada por su envidia que lleva al suicidio.*

*Aunque Lorca no confirma que Adela esté embarazada, no se puede negar que la escena final del segundo acto nos permite conjeturar que lo está, y hay una amplia gama de ejemplos, como cuando les pide a sus hermanas que no salgan y que dejen escapar a la hija de la Librada: "(Cogiéndose el vientre.) ¡No! ¡No!". Me limitaría a señalar que esto aumentaría su desesperación porque sin Pepe ella sería una madre soltera, como la hija de la Librada.*

*En conclusión, la muerte de Adela es inevitable porque no puede luchar contra su madre y porque cree que nunca podrá escapar de la casa ni encontrar la felicidad sin el amor de su vida. Y no hay que olvidar que Angustias le robó a su Pepe, ya que ella tuvo una relación con él un año antes. Además ¿Qué futuro podría tener una madre soltera en la casa de Bernarda Alba?*

A clear introduction which lays out the format of the essay.

Good explanation of the first point, in spite of some unnecessary repetition (*'el hombre que ama... está enamorada'*). The quotation is pertinent and poetic.

Good expansion of the second point but lacking analysis. Another example of the conflict between mother and daughter would have reinforced the point.

Relationship with other sisters would have been beneficial as well as another quotation.

Although difficult to substantiate, this supposition is a good addition and has been well supported, adding depth and analysis. However, there are a succession of 'exam phrases' like: *me limitaría a señalar, no se puede negar que ...*, which lack spontaneity and sound rehearsed.

The conclusion successfully summarises what has happened but unfortunately adds a new point which should have been developed beforehand. The final rhetorical question is a good stylistic ending.

This is a middle-of-the-road essay. It has a cohesive structure and the ideas flow. The second half of the question is only tackled in the conclusion and should have been developed in greater detail earlier. The language and grammar have some sophisticated elements, for example, good manipulation of verb tenses and moods.

## Plot and Structure

**Actividad 4** *(page 14)*

**1**d, **2**f, **3**a, **4**e, **5**c, **6**b

**Actividad 8** *(page 18)*

**a**3, **b**8, **c**6, **d**7, **e**1, **f**2, **g**4, **h**5

**Actividad 10** *(page 19)*

**1**b desarrolla, **2**e hacen, **3**d habla, **4**k recuerda, **5**l vuelven, **6**c envidia, **7**a anuncia, **8**i interviene, **9**f golpea, **10**h insiste, **11**g identifica, **12**j quiere

## Characters

**Actividad 1** *(page 45)*

**1**f, **2**g, **3**j, **4**h, **5**i, **6**a, **7**b, **8**c, **9**e, **10**d

**Actividad 3** *(page 49)*

**1**o, **2/3**a/i either order, **4**n, **5**f, **6**d, **7**c, **8**k, **9**h, **10**b

**Actividad 6** *(page 54)*

**1**j, **2**g, **3**i, **4**a, **5**h, **6**c, **7**e, **8**b, **9**d, **10**f

**Actividad 7** *(page 55)*

**1**g, **2**f, **3**c, **4**j, **5**d, **6**i, **7**h, **8**b, **9**e, **10**a

**Actividad 8** *(page 56)*

**1**c, **2**e, **3**d, **4**b, **5**a

**Actividad 9** *(page 57)*

**1**h, **2**g or f, **3**j, **4**b, **5**f or g, **6**i, **7**a, **8**e, **9**d, **10**c

## Language

**Actividad 2** *(page 66)*

**1**a, **2**c, **3**e, **4**d, **5**b

**Actividad 6** *(page 74)*

**a** F/ **b** V/ **c** V/ **d** V/ **e** V/ **f** V/ **g** F/ **h** F/ **i** V/ **j** N

## Themes

**Actividad 2** *(page 84)*

**a**6, **b**5, **c**7, **d**1, **e**2, **f**3, **g**4, **h**8

**Actividad 7** *(page 88)*

**a** tengo que, **b** insoportable, **c** la falta de, **d** dejó, **e** ir a misa, **f** dijo, **g** vigilaba, **h** el hombre más guapo, **i** dejar de, **j** me dio mucha lástima

# Glossary

**agricultural sector** ***el sector agrícola*** the area of economic activity concerned with cultivating land, raising crops, feeding and raising livestock and farming

**anarchist movement** ***el movimiento anarquista*** a political movement calling for the end of law and government restraint on society

**antagonist** ***el/la antagonista*** a person who actively opposes or is hostile to someone or something

**antipathy** ***la antipatía*** a feeling of intense aversion, dislike, or hostility

**antithesis** ***la antítesis*** the direct opposite of something/someone

**avant-garde** ***vanguardista*** new and experimental ideas and methods in art, music, or literature

**ballad** ***el romance*** a poem or song which tells a story, usually written in short stanzas

**betrothed** ***el/la prometido/a*** someone who is engaged to marry

**el cante jondo** ***deep song*** a traditional vocal style of flamenco music

**catalyst** ***el catalizador*** a person or thing that brings about change

**climax** ***el climax*** the decisive moment in a plot

**constitution** ***la constitución*** a set of political principles by which a country is governed

**courtship** ***el cortejo*** the act (by one person) of trying to win the favourable attention of another, especially by a man towards a woman

**dictatorship** ***la dictadura*** a country, government, or the form of government in which absolute power is exercised by one person (the dictator)

**documentary** ***el documental*** a factual account of an event or person presenting the facts with little or no fiction

**double entendre** ***el doble sentido*** a word or phrase open to two different interpretations, one of which is usually risqué

**dowry** ***la dote*** the money and goods that a wife brings to her husband at marriage

**eponymous** ***epónimo*** the person after whom a literary work/film is named

**exile** ***el exilio*** a person who is banished or separated from his or her native land

**exposition** ***la exposición*** dialogue or description that gives the audience or reader the background of the characters and the present situation

**façade** ***la fachada*** a deceptive outward appearance; also the main front/face of a house

**falling action** ***el acción decreciente*** the part of a literary plot that occurs after the climax has been reached and the conflict has been resolved.

**foreshadowing** ***el presagio*** a warning of a future event

**hierarchy** ***la jerarquía*** any system of persons or things ranked one above another

**industrial revolution** ***la revolución industrial*** the totality of the changes in economic and social organisation that began in about 1760 in England and later in other countries, characterised chiefly by the replacement of hand tools with power-driven machines

***La Falange*** Fascist political movement

**last response** ***el último responso*** the final part of a church service of Mass

**mantilla** ***la mantilla*** a lace or silk scarf worn by women over the head and shoulders

**martyr** ***el mártir*** someone who deliberately invites or exaggerates suffering to gain sympathy; someone who suffers and dies for their faith

**matriarch** ***la matriarca*** the female head of a household; an older woman with power or influence in a family

**mourning** ***el luto*** the conventional signs of sorrow for a person's death, especially wearing black, not leaving the house except to go to church

**naïve** ***un/una ingenuo/a*** a person showing a lack of experience, wisdom, or judgement; gullible

**Nationalist party** ***el Partido Nacionalista*** political group advocating or fighting for national independence, a strong national government or federalism (where provinces share power with central government)

**omnipresent** ***omnipresente*** present everywhere

**oneiric** ***onírico*** relating to dreams

**pealing of bells** ***el doblar de las campanas*** when church bells are rung

**posthumously** ***póstumamente*** after death

**protagonist** ***el/la protagonista*** the leading character of a drama or other piece of writing

**reapers** ***los segadores*** men who gather the harvest

**resolution** ***el desenlace*** the conclusion of the literary plot

**rising action** ***el nudo*** a related series of incidents in a literary plot that build toward the point of greatest interest

**risqué** ***atrevido*** daringly close to indelicacy or impropriety

**rosary** ***el rosario*** a series of Catholic prayers repeated in a set order, often using rosary beads to keep track of the prayers

**secularisation** ***la secularización*** the removal of religious authority

**socialist values** ***los valores socialistas*** left-wing values in which the means of production and distribution of goods are owned and controlled by social groups or by the government, rather than by private business

**stage directions** ***las acotaciones*** instructions to an actor or director, written into the script of a play

**stallion** ***el caballo garañón*** an uncastrated adult male horse, especially one used for breeding

**status quo** ***statu quo*** the existing state of affairs

**stylised** ***estilizado*** presented in a non-realistic way

**subjugation** ***el sometimiento*** the act of bringing someone under complete control

**suitor** ***el pretendiente*** a potential partner/spouse

**surreal** ***surrealista*** seemingly unreal

**surrealism** ***el surrealismo*** a movement focused on releasing the subconscious mind to find new levels of creativity; often using images and words in unconventional ways

**symbol** ***el símbolo*** an object used to represent an idea, often an important theme in the story

**trousseau** ***el ajuar*** a collection of belongings women take with them on marriage, including clothes and linen for their new home; usually which they will sew themselves

**tyranny** ***la tiranía*** the use of power that has no limits or bounds; abuse of power

OXFORD
UNIVERSITY PRESS

Great Clarendon Street, Oxford, OX2 6DP, United Kingdom

Oxford University Press is a department of the University of Oxford. It furthers the University's objective of excellence in research, scholarship, and education by publishing worldwide. Oxford is a registered trade mark of Oxford University Press in the UK and in certain other countries.


First published in 2017



British Library Cataloguing in Publication Data

Data available

ISBN 978-019-841836-8

Kindle edition ISBN 978-0-19-841829-0

10 9 8

Printed and bound by CPI Group (UK) Ltd, Croydon, CR0 4YY

**Acknowledgements**

The publisher and authors would like to thank the following for permission to use photographs and other copyright material:

Extracts from the Bloomsbury Methuen Drama edition of La casa de Bernarda Alba, 2007, © The Estate of Federico García Lorca

**Cover:** Tasha1111/iStockphoto; **p10:** Timaginas Teatro/Raúl Guadarrama; **p12:** Robbie Jack - Corbis/Getty Images; **p13:** criben/Shutterstock; **p25:** Timaginas Teatro/Raúl Guadarrama; **p30:** M Ramírez/Alamy Stock Photo; **p32:** World History Archive/Alamy Stock Photo; **p34:** Marta Cobos/Shutterstock; **p39:** Granger Historical Picture Archive/Alamy Stock Photo; **p46:** Moviestore collection Ltd/Alamy Stock Photo; **p42:** Ed-Ni Photo/Shutterstock; **p50:** criben/Shutterstock; **p53:** Timaginas Teatro/Raúl Guadarrama; **p55:** Courtesy of Estudio Corazza; **p62:** Timaginas Teatro/Raúl Guadarrama; **p67:** Robbie Jack - Corbis/Getty Images; **p68:** tcsaba/Shutterstock; **p76:** Moviestore collection Ltd/Alamy Stock Photo; **p80:** Timaginas Teatro/Raúl Guadarrama; **p81:** Callipso/Shutterstock; **p83, 90:** criben/ Shutterstock.

Every effort has been made to contact copyright holders of material reproduced in this book. Any omissions will be rectified in subsequent printings if notice is given to the publisher.